prettylittlepincushions

prettylittlepincushions

LARK BOOKS

A Division of Sterling Publishing Co., Inc.
New York / London

EDITOR:
SUSAN BRILL

ART DIRECTOR:
DANA IRWIN

DEVELOPMENT EDITORS:
NICOLE MCCONVILLE
AND MARTHE LE VAN

COVER DESIGNER:
CINDY LABREACHT

ASSOCIATE ART DIRECTORS:
CHRIS BRYANT,
ROBIN GREGORY,
AVERY JOHNSON,
BRADLEY NORRIS,
KRISTI PFEFFER,
LANCE WILLE, AND
SHANNON YOKELEY

ART PRODUCTION ASSISTANT:
JEFF HAMILTON

EDITORIAL ASSISTANCE:
JULIE HALE,
CASSIE MOORE,
AND MARK BLOOM

ILLUSTRATORS:
SUSAN MCBRIDE AND
ORRIN LUNDGREN

PHOTOGRAPHER:
JOHN WIDMAN

Library of Congress Cataloging-in-Publication Data

Pretty little pincushions / [Susan Brill, ed.]. -- 1st ed.
  p. cm.
 Includes index.
 ISBN-13: 978-1-60059-144-0 (hc-plc with jacket : alk. paper)
 ISBN-10: 1-60059-144-2 (hc-plc with jacket : alk. paper)
 1. Pincushions. I. Brill, Susan.
 TT899.3.P74 2007
 745.5--dc22
                                                   2007018423

10 9 8 7 6 5 4 3 2

First Edition

Published by Lark Books, A Division of
Sterling Publishing Co., Inc.
387 Park Avenue South, New York, N.Y. 10016

Text © 2007, Lark Books
Photography © 2007
Illustrations © 2007

Distributed in Canada by Sterling Publishing,
c/o Canadian Manda Group, 165 Dufferin Street
Toronto, Ontario, Canada M6K 3H6

Distributed in the United Kingdom by GMC Distribution Services,
Castle Place, 166 High Street, Lewes, East Sussex, England BN7 1XU

Distributed in Australia by Capricorn Link (Australia) Pty Ltd.,
P.O. Box 704, Windsor, NSW 2756 Australia

If you have questions or comments about this book, please contact:
Lark Books, 67 Broadway, Asheville, NC 28801
828-253-0467

Manufactured in China

ISBN 13: 978-1-60059-144-0
ISBN 10: 1-60059-144-2

For information about custom editions, special sales, premium and corporate purchases, please
contact Sterling Special Sales Department at 800-805-5489 or specialsales@sterlingpub.com.

table of contents

Introduction 6

Pincushion Basics 8

Chapter One: Sitting Pretty 22
  Wild Strawberries 24
  Corsage Pins 27
  Close-Knit Friends 30
  Fruitful Day 32
  Cute & Curious 35
  Star Dust 38
  Bee Sewing 40
  Sunny-Side Up 43
  Designs on Felt 46
  Sweet Dreams 51
  Timeless Treasures 54

Chapter Two: Sew Nostalgic 58
  Feminine Mystique 60
  Elegant Notions 62
  Whipstitich It Good 65
  Twisted Lids 67
  Dress It Up 70

Kitchen Stitchin' 73
No-Sew Kitch 76
Creative Edge 78
Off the Cuff Creatures 80

Chapter Three: Pretty & Petite 84
  At Your Fingertips 86
  Sew on the Go 88
  Spin the Bottlecap 90

Chapter Four: Pincushion or Plushie? 98
  On Pins and Needles 100
  Ruling the Roost 103
  Pin Pals 106
  Tropical Splash 109
  Feeling Needled 112
  Pinning Zoo 114

Designer Bios 116
Acknowledgments 118
Templates 119
Metric Equivalents Chart 128
Index 128

PRETTY
Pincushions
LITTLE

Introduction

desperate for an antidote to the mass-marketed mass production of modern life? Crafters everywhere have seized on a radical response: sit yourself down and stitch up something personalized and pretty.

That's right, *pretty*. It's back, minus the doilies and frills, and full of attitude. The ruffles and bunnies of pretty past have given way to girly-and-proud-of-it accents of all kinds, from embroidered pop-art flowers to felt appliqués in flirty designs and bright colors.

And let's face it. If you're looking for a symbol of simpler times to celebrate and decorate in post-modern pretty style, you can't top that beloved icon of domesticity, the pincushion. It has nostalgic appeal that's unmistakable and makeover readiness that's irresistible. Click on any popular crafting site to see that pincushions are only too willing to transcend their humble station in the sewing basket and emerge as the perfect mini-canvas for showcasing fabulous fabrics, whimsical embellishments, playful ideas, clever new techniques, and, most important, individual style.

Some of the most talented and inventive designers working in needlecrafts today accepted our invitation to rummage through their fabric stashes, pull out their favorite baubles and trims, and create enchantingly original pincushion projects. The results—30 beginner-

friendly designs—run the full range of pretty, from ultra-femme to vintage chic, classic luxe to quirky charm.

You'll find traditional fruit shapes stitched from luminous quilted silk, colorful rounds of printed fabric accented with antique ribbon and buttons, pillowy velvet squares studded with elegant seed beads, and an adorable menagerie of ladybugs, porcupines, and other plushie-style creatures—even a cuddly pair of cacti complete with pins as spines. Proving that pretty is, indeed, as pretty does, there's also a flower corsage bracelet pincushion, a darling heart-shaped ring cushion, a sweet on-the-go sewing kit topped with a tiny pincushion lid, and retro-cute pincushions popping out of flea-market teacups.

These little pretties are a perfect excuse to use fabric scraps you've been saving for something special, experiment with an embellishment technique you've been dying to try, or perfect your own trademark stitch or accent. They also lend themselves beautifully to experimentation, variation, and quick and easy multiples for the loveliest mini-presents ever.

In other words, they're just what you were looking for. So go ahead, pick up a needle and thread and join the revolution.

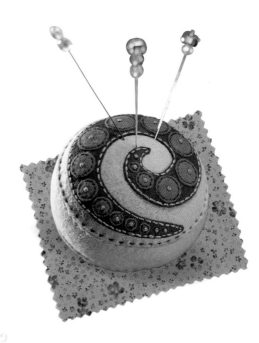

pincushionbasics

his chapter gives you background on materials, tools, and techniques for sewing the projects in this book. Whether you're an experienced sewer or a novice, be sure to look through this chapter before you begin. Most projects call for the Basic Pincushion Tool Kit, so gather those items, listed on the following page, before you start. Then, breeze through the Tools section and Materials section so you know what you're in for. Take note of the illustrated hand-sewing stitches in this section, too. You may need to flip back and reference it for a stitch in your project. (Or you may read it just for fun to learn a new technique. What a stitch!)

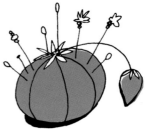

Chances are, you have all of the supplies you need for these projects right in your sewing basket, or not too far away. From fabric remnants to extra buttons and leftover trim, you'll find a use for all of those scraps in these pretty little pincushions.

basic pincushion tool kit

- Sharp sewing scissors (for fabric)
- Sharp fine-tipped scissors (for detailed work)
- Craft scissors (for paper)
- Measuring tape
- Straight pins
- Hand-sewing needles
- Thread
- Large-eyed embroidery needle
- Embroidery floss (as specified in each project)
- Polyester fiberfill
- Scrap paper (for patterns)
- Pencil with an eraser (for drawing and stuffing, both)
- Seam ripper
- Rice, lentils, or sand (for weight) and a small funnel

pincushion tools

SHARP SEWING SCISSORS

Find these at a fabric store. Sharp, quality scissors will last a long time and will make a noticeable difference when cutting fabric. Never (ever) use this fine pair for cutting paper! The wood fibers of paper will dull the blades quickly and render them useless on fabric.

Some projects also call for fine-tipped sewing scissors, which are a smaller pair used for cutting tight curves and detailed work. Also keep these pristine for cutting only fabric or thread.

CRAFT SCISSORS

Craft scissors need cut only paper in these projects, so a cheap, affordable pair is fine. You'll want a short-to-moderate length to make fine cuts on pattern curves and corners.

TIP | TWO-SCISSOR DAY

Most of these are two-scissor projects—cut the pattern from scrap paper with craft scissors, and cut the fabric with sewing scissors.

HAND-SEWING NEEDLES

A variety pack of needles will likely include everything you need for the projects in this book. Choose a finer needle for lightweight fabrics and a thicker, longer needle for thicker fabrics. Here are some of the differences:

Sharps

Use sharp pointed needles, or "sharps," for all of these projects unless otherwise noted. Regular woven fabrics do best with sharp needles; silk especially requires a sharp point.

Ball-Point Needles

Round-tipped, or "ball point," needles (and pins) are best for knit materials. The ball point pushes between the fabric fibers rather than piercing through a fiber, which can cause a run or pull in the weave of a knit.

Embroidery Needles

Some of these projects call specifically for an embroidery needle for detailing. This needle has a longer eye for ease in threading multiple strands of floss at once but can be used for regular hand stitching as well.

NEEDLE THREADER

Many needle packs will also include a needle threader—a fine loop of wire attached to a small holder. Don't set this funny little piece aside! You can lick and twist the ends of your thread indefinitely, trying to get that one renegade fraying fiber through the eye of your needle, or you can use this handy tool. The stiff, thin wire easily goes through the eye of just about any needle. Simply put it through the needle, insert the thread in the (very generous) wire loop, and pull the wire back through the needle. The wire carries the thread back with it, threading the needle.

STRAIGHT PINS

Short metal pins with tiny heads will do the job for these projects, but longer ones with plastic or glass heads are easier to handle and easier to see. And, therefore, easier to remove (for fewer unexpected pin pokes).

Even better, don't settle for plain old pins. It's so easy to embellish your own with beads and permanent glue (see Embellishing Pins, page 83), or use shrink plastic to cut and color shapes to any theme (see Bee Pins, page 42), and crown your pins with personality.

SEAM RIPPER

Indispensable. We all make mistakes, and it's much faster to undo them with a seam ripper than scissors or (heaven forbid) a straight pin when the stitches are too small for scissors.

optional tools

SEWING MACHINE

Some of these projects call for a sewing machine, but—never fear—it's optional. Every one of these charming crafts can be stitched by hand if you prefer. If you sew with a machine, use a longer stitch for thicker fabrics, and reduce the pressure on the presser foot a bit to allow fabric to move easily through the machine. Use a zigzag stitch on raw edges to keep fabrics from raveling.

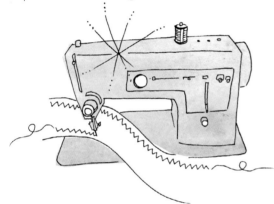

SEWING MACHINE NEEDLES

Sewing machine needles are inexpensive, so always have extras on hand. You may break one sewing through many thicknesses of fabric in one of these projects. Or, if you nick a lot of pins while sewing, your needle will become dull. It's a good rule of thumb to start each sewing project with a new needle.

TIP LESSEN THE PRESSURE

When sewing thick layers, like felt, you may need to reduce your presser foot pressure for the layers to move easily through the sewing machine. Just be sure to readjust it again for sewing skimpier fabric.

ROTARY CUTTER

A rotary cutter makes cutting a breeze. Use a cutting mat and a ruler with this tool. Hold the cutter at a 45° angle, making sure the blade is set firmly against the ruler's edge. Keep an even pressure on the cutter, and always cut away from yourself. Keep the guard over the blade when you're not cutting.

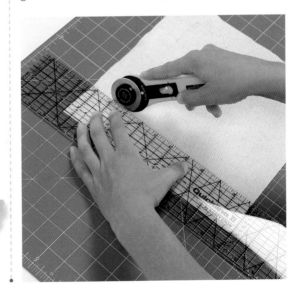

pincushionmaterials

THREADS

Resist (indeed, boycott) the three-for-a-dollar bargain bin of thread. Instead, buy a quality polyester thread for your machine sewing and hand sewing. It will create a stronger seam than bargain thread and be light and thin enough to pass through the fabric with the greatest of ease. Unless otherwise noted, use thread that matches the fabric for your pincushion project.

FLOSSES

Embroidery floss is a decorative thread that comes in six loosely twisted strands. It's available in cotton, silk,

rayon, or other fibers, and in a vast array of colors for every needlework application. Several strands can be used at once with an embroidery needle for sewing decorative stitches. These projects use one strand of floss at a time, unless otherwise indicated.

NAPS AND WEAVES

The majority of these projects call for felt, but you can step up your design with other fabrics too. Use scraps from sewing or repurpose a swatch from a favorite shirt or pair of pants. Some projects—such as the funky chicken in Ruling the Roost, made from toe socks—call for a knit fabric, but for most projects you'll want a material that doesn't give, something sturdy to hold the pincushion's shape as you stash your pins. Here's a brief description of the differences in fabric content:

Cotton

Cotton is a natural choice for crafts because it's easy to sew and comes in a seemingly limitless array of colors and prints. Cotton's strengths are durability, density, and drape. A medium-weight cotton will hold your pincushion together in fine form. And, in this application, you don't need to worry about cotton's limitations of shrinking and wrinkling. (If you foresee the need to sew a washable pincushion, however, then do preshrink your fabric.)

Linen

With its lustrous fibers from the flax plant, linen is more expensive than cotton but offers the same advantages.

It comes in weights from handkerchief to suiting; it's strong and durable (even stronger wet than dry, in case your pincushion takes an inadvertent dunk in the sink one day); and it comes in an array of wonderful colors and prints as well. Linen, however, is so prone to wrinkling that even stuffing the pincushion firmly probably can't straighten out all of the wrinkles. So, press your fabric well before (and after) sewing to have a smooth, unwrinkled surface for your finished pincushion.

Silk

While linen is lustrous, silk is just plain luxurious. Since it's an expensive fabric, use the scraps and remnants you have from other sewing projects to make the most of your pricey investment. Silk is damaged by overexposure to sunlight and by oils. Keep sewing machine oil (and potato chips) away from your silk project.

Felt

Wonder why so many craft projects call for felt? Because it's a wonder fabric. It's non-woven, doesn't ravel, is soft and cuddly, and has no right side or wrong side. What could be easier? Traditionally made from wool, synthetic felt is also available. For a real back-to-basics experience, felt your own wool from an old sweater or a thrift-store find. Find instructions for felting on page 17.

Wool

Wool can be fuzzy or smooth, fleecy or ribbed. It's soft and durable and very absorbent. Like silk, it can be damaged by excessive exposure to sunlight. It's another great fabric for sewing. When reusing wool for crafts, be sure to clean it thoroughly. Any stains and perspiration on the fabric are a draw to moths who lay their eggs in wool's cozy fibers, which the moth larvae then love to feed on.

STUFFINGS

Polyester fiberfill is the designated stuffing for most of these projects. But you may prefer cotton batting or wool roving (wool fiber used for felting and spinning). Take your pick.

Polyester fiberfill will keep its shape well. Grade one variety is brand new, soft, and fibrous. It's resilient and non-allergenic, and readily available at craft and sewing stores. Grade two is more coarse, has more bounce than grade one stuffing, and is more environmentally friendly than the other (since it's not all new material), but it's usually available only in bulk. Ask your craft or fabric store if they carry it.

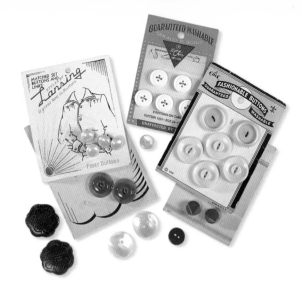

TIP MOM'S BUDGET STUFFING

Instead of throwing away hosiery with runs, crafty moms in the 1970s used to wash it and save the legs (minus the super-tight control top section) for stuffing pillows and crafts. The sky's the limit on what you can use to stuff your pincushions on a budget!

WEIGHTING MATERIALS

Many of these projects also call for lentils, rice, or sand to weight your pincushion. The clever Cute and Curious mouse project (page 35) calls for a river rock, so that little guy will sit up straight and not go scampering around your table. The weighting material is put at the bottom of the cushion, usually after the fluffy stuffing—whichever type you choose.

EMBELLISHMENTS

This is where the pincushion really becomes you! Whether it's for your own sewing pleasure or a great gift for a friend, go creatively crazy with beads, buttons, and baubles to dress your pincushion. These projects give endless ways to trim the pincushions with embroidery stitches and felt flowers.

You can also repurpose trim and decoration from old clothes, or gather hip and trendy accouterments to top them off.

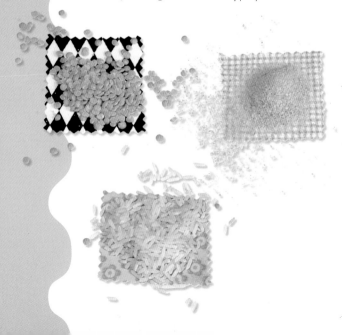

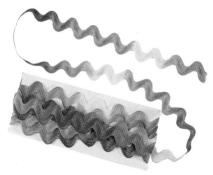

basic techniques

CLIPPING CURVES AND CORNERS

When you sew a pincushion inside out, all of the material in the seam allowance on a curve will bunch together when turned right side out. To help it find its own space and lay flat, snip about two-thirds of the way into the seam allowance in several places on the curve. This allows the fabric to overlap slightly where it was snipped and results in a smoother curve and seam on the right side.

The same is true of the fabric on a corner. When turned right side out, it will fold on itself to try to fit into the close confines of the corner. Before turning right side out, clip straight across the corner of the seam allowance, halfway between the stitching and the corner of the fabric. (In a project that will be stuffed, don't cut too close to the stitching, or it will weaken the corner and be the first place to burst open under pressure.)

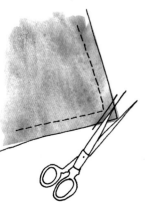

pincushions past

THE ART OF STUFFING

Take time to stuff your pincushions carefully— using small bits of stuffing for a smoother fill. Use the eraser end of a pencil, which will grip the stuffing nicely to scoot it around just where you need it in corners and hard-to-reach places. Or, use a chopstick, a knitting needle, the blunt end of scissors, or any long, thin, pointed (but not too pointed) tool you have. Fill gently but firmly, and don't overstuff, or your pincushion will be bursting at the seams.

A WEIGHTIER PINCUSHION

To add weight to your pincushion, leave the gap for stuffing at the bottom of the pincushion. Stuff it three-quarters full with polyester fiberfill, and then top it off with rice or lentils—about $1/4$ cup, depending on the size of your pincushion. Close the gap securely with hand stitching to keep the rice or lentils contained.

This pincushion is stuffed with polyester fiberfill. Rice is added for weight.

LOSING THE THREAD

It's easy to hide the tail ("lose the thread") of a knotted thread on a stuffed project. Make the knot at the last stitch, but don't cut the thread. Instead, push the threaded needle through the stuffed body to the opposite side. Press in on the stuffing a bit and pull the thread tight, cutting it close to the fabric. When the stuffing expands back into form, the thread is pulled inside the cushion—hidden from view. (If the tip of the thread still shows, use your needle to gently pick at the outer layer of felt, raising it up to sink the tip of the thread beneath.)

TUFTING

Tufting is a technique to create gathers on a cushioned surface. A pillow with a button in the center that cinches the center front to the center back is an example of tufting. One way to tuft a pincushion is to push the needle into the bottom and out the top in the center, leaving a tail of thread at the bottom of the pincushion. On the top, sew through a button, if desired, or simply return the needle through the top center back to the bottom center. On the bottom, pull both threads tightly, dimpling, or tufting, the top and bottom of the cushion, and tie in a tight knot.

FELTING

Felted wool has a wonderfully rich texture, is a sturdy fabric, and doesn't ravel. Felting vintage sweaters from your local thrift shop ensures a one-of-a-kind look for any of the designs in this book calling for felt.

Felted wool is created by washing knit wool, such as a sweater, in hot water and drying it with the hot setting in a clothes dryer. The wool fibers join together and shrink. If your wool ravels slightly after felting, simply sew a zig-zag stitch with a sewing machine along the cut edges to prevent further raveling.

100% wool sweater swatch

Selecting a Sweater to Felt
The felting process will drastically shrink a sweater, so purchase one of ample size for your needs.

Choose sweaters made of 100 percent wool. Sweaters of 100 percent lamb's wool, cashmere, and wool/angora blends also work, but may require multiple runs through

Same swatch as above, felted

the washing machine. You can also felt sweaters made from a wool blend containing less than 10 percent acrylic/nylon fiber. The bulkier the knit, the rougher and thicker the felted

fabric. So, keep in mind the use for your felt and the thickness of fabric you can feasibly use.

The Felting Process
Remove any zippers and buttons before beginning the felting process.

1 Using the hottest setting on your washing machine, place the sweater and some liquid laundry detergent in the washer. Allow the washer to run completely through its cycle.

2 When the cycle is complete, check the felting process. If the sweater stretches easily, or the stitches are still easily visible, repeat the washing process. In some cases, you will need to repeat the washing process several times.

3 When the sweater is sufficiently felted, hang it up to dry. It will be very small! Using the dryer will hasten the felting, but on regular wool it also adds a significantly rougher texture. If you use the dryer, be sure to remove the sweater promptly when the dryer is done.

4 To turn the very small, felted sweater into useable swatches of felted wool, cut it into four pieces: First remove the arms at the shoulders; then cut the front and back into two separate pieces, working along the existing seams. Turn the sweater inside out to see the seams, if necessary.

*pincushions*past

TIP FELTED RAVEL
If your felted sweater ravels slightly when you cut it, simply sew a zigzag stitch with a sewing machine along the cut edges to prevent further raveling.

HAND-SEWING STITCHES

All of the projects in this book can be made by hand sewing with a needle and thread. In case you're not familiar with one of the stitches or knots in your project, they're illustrated here for reference:

Backstitch

The backstitch is a hand-stitching method for creating a seam, and it's a good one for stuffed projects, holding the seam under pressure (figure 1).

Basting Stitch

Basting is a means to temporarily secure two edges of fabric where a seam is intended to go. This stitch is the same as a running stitch, but with very long stitches that are easily removed after the permanent seam is in place (see Running Stitch).

Blanket Stitch

The blanket stitch is a decorative (and functional) technique for accentuating an edge or attaching a cut shape to a layer of fabric (figure 2).

Blind Stitch

This stitch is, as it sounds, meant to be invisible. It's sewn by taking very small horizontal stitches in the fabric so the thread is visible on the wrong side, but virtually invisible on the right side of the fabric (figure 3).

Buttonhole Stitch

The buttonhole stitch is similar to the blanket stitch, but forms a knot at the fabric edge (figure 4).

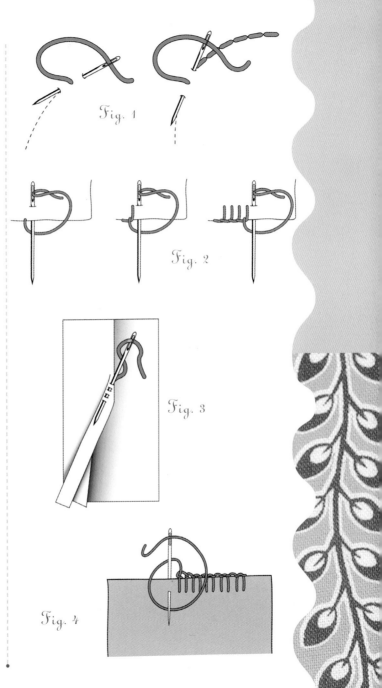

Fig. 1

Fig. 2

Fig. 3

Fig. 4

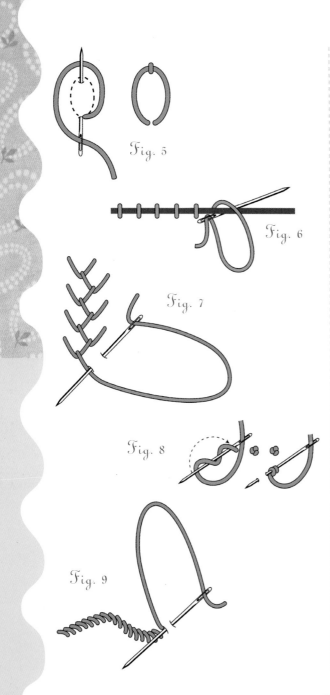

Fig. 5

Fig. 6

Fig. 7

Fig. 8

Fig. 9

Chain Stitch

Work this stitch in a circle to form a flower (figure 5). It's also called the Lazy Daisy stitch.

Couching Stitch

A traditional couching stitch uses two threads and two needles. One thread is laid in position on the fabric and the other thread is stitched over it to hold it in place. The stitching thread is sewn in evenly spaced stitches at right angles to the other thread (figure 6).

Feather Stitch

This stitch creates a feathery line that is used for smocking and quilting. It's a great stitch that's effective when sewn in a straight line or following a curve (figure 7).

French Knot

This elegant knot is used for embellishment and is meant to show (figure 8)!

Outline Stitch

This is the same as the stem stitch, but with the thread worked to the left of the needle (figure 9).

Overcast Stitch

See Whipstitch.

Running Stitch

This stitch is as basic as it sounds—a single thread drawn in a straight line made by weaving the needle through the fabric at evenly spaced intervals (figure 10). It's used for sewing a drawstring to gather fabric together.

Satin Stitch

The satin stitch is composed of parallel rows of straight stitches, often to fill in an outline (figure 11).

Straight Stitch

Use a simple straight stitch to create a motif (figure 12).

Stem Stitch

This is also known as a crewel stitch and is often sewn to outline a shape (figure 13).

Surgeon's Knot

This knot resists slipping and is great for temporarily tying off the thread of an unfinished seam while you stop to stuff your pincushion (figure 14).

Whipstitch

The whipstitch is a hand stitch used for binding edges to prevent raveling (figure 15). Sew the stitches over the edge of the fabric. It's also called an overcast stitch.

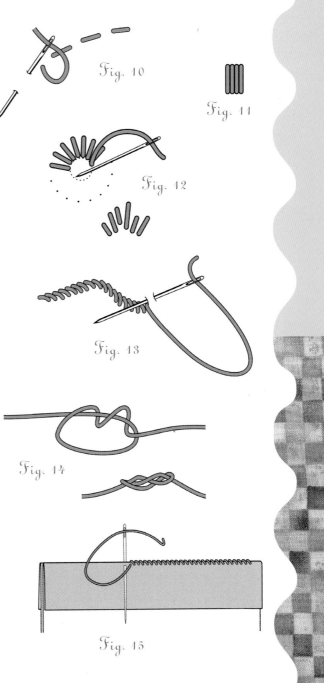

Fig. 10

Fig. 11

Fig. 12

Fig. 13

Fig. 14

Fig. 15

sitting pretty

Fetching and functional,
these cushions have it all.

23

wildstrawberries

The classic strawberry pincushion gets updated with a sprinkling of sequins and cool green leaves. Each button blossom—an extra-crafty addition—contains a needle book.

DESIGNER

ANGELA BATE

WHAT YOU NEED

Basic Pincushion Tool Kit (page 9)

Wool felt, 2 greens, red, yellow, white

Sewing machine (optional)

2 vintage buttons

Embroidery floss, red, green, white

Ribbon, green

Sequins

Pinking shears

Glue stick

strawberry pincushion

WHAT YOU DO

1   Make a pattern from the template (page 119), and cut out the strawberry on the fold of the red felt.

2   Machine stitch or hand sew the long edge with a small $\frac{1}{8}$-inch seam allowance, leaving the top of the berry unsewn. Reinforce the ends of the seam. Turn the berry right side out and firmly stuff with polyester fiberfill.

3 Hand sew a running stitch around the top. Pull both ends of the thread like a drawstring to gather the top.

4 Cut a 6-inch piece of green ribbon. Insert both ends of the ribbon into the gathered top of the berry, and stitch tightly closed.

5 Randomly sew on sequins for seeds, hiding your knot inside the gathered end of the berry.

6 Cut three of each leaf pattern, or any combination, for a total of six large leaves in the green felts. Attach them to the top of the berry with a running stitch down the center of the leaf. Position them to overlap slightly and cover the gathers on the strawberry, surrounding the ribbon.

blossom needle book

1 Make a pattern from the template (page 119), and cut out three circles of white felt with the pinking shears. Cut two leaves of coordinating greens and two yellow blossoms with straight scissors.

2 Stitch a vintage button to each flower center with red embroidery floss. Hand stitch lines at random around the flower center with embroidery floss. Set aside.

3 Cut a 4-inch piece of green ribbon and form it into a loop. Stack the three circles of white felt together, inserting leaves and the ribbon loop into the sides.

4 Machine stitch (or hand sew) in a straight line across one side of the flower, as noted on the pattern. Sew through all of the thicknesses.

5 Glue flower blossoms to the front and back of the needle book with a glue stick. Stock the needle book with a few choice needles to meet every need—at least one fine needle, a medium weight, and a large-eyed one.

corsagepins

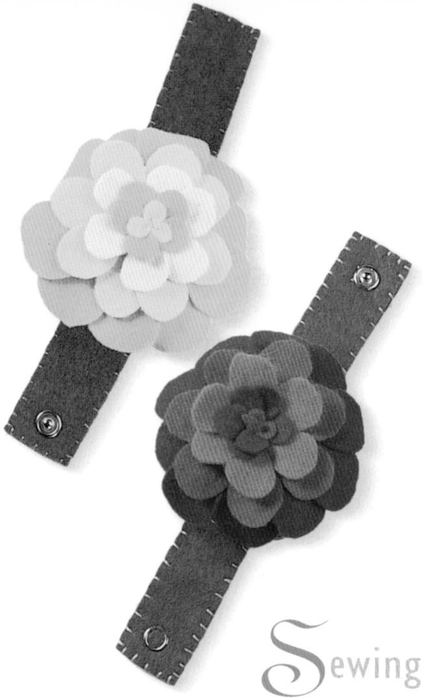

Sewing a big project is a snap with this sunshiny wrist corsage. Fasten it in place, and your pins won't get buried under patterns and prints as you work.

DESIGNER

CASSI GRIFFIN

WHAT YOU NEED

- Basic Pincushion Tool Kit (page 9)
- Wool felt, green, three shades of yellow
- Embroidery floss, matching colors
- Acetate or cardboard
- Snap and snap tool, or hook and loop tape

WHAT YOU DO

1 Create a pattern from the template (page 120), and cut the pincushion pieces from felt as follows: Petal A, cut 10 in dark yellow; Petal B, cut eight in medium yellow; Petal C, cut six in light yellow; Petal D, cut five in dark yellow; and Petal E, cut three in medium yellow. Cut two of the Pincushion piece from green, and cut one of the plastic insert from the acetate. Cut the band, wrist strap, and tab from green.

2 Stitch the short sides of the tab to the center of the pincushion back using running stitches and two strands of green floss.

3 To make the wrist strap, apply one half of the snap to one strap. Apply the other half of the snap to the other strap. Place the straps with wrong sides together, with straps at opposite ends and on opposite sides. Blanket stitch the two wrist straps together using three strands of green floss and the embroidery needle. Set aside.

4 To create the pincushion top, overlap the Petal A pieces in a circle on the outer edge of the pincushion top piece. Position them to overhang the edge by half. Whipstitch each in place at its center using two strands of yellow floss.

5 Position each consecutive round of petals inside and overlapping the last set (see at right). Stitch each round in place in the same manner. Place the last round of petals directly on top of the previous round, alternating spacing, and stitch in place.

6 Using three strands of green floss, blanket stitch the side-band to the pincushion top. Tuck under each edge, and use small running stitches to secure the edges to the pincushion.

7 Stitch the pincushion bottom onto the other side of the pincushion band using 3 strands of green floss in a blanket stitch. At the halfway point, stop and place the plastic insert inside, on the bottom. Continue stitching. Leave a 1½-inch opening for stuffing.

8 Stuff firmly with polyester fiberfill between the top of the pincushion and the plastic insert. Then stitch the opening closed. Slide the strap through the tab on the back of the pincushion.

TIP **ACETATE ALTERNATIVE**
If you don't have plastic acetate on hand for the plastic insert, use anything that will keep pins from poking through to your wrist—cut a disc from the plastic lid of a yogurt container, for example.

close-knitfriends

*P*reserve and repurpose the wool from a favorite sweater with these charming pincushions.

DESIGNER

JOAN K. MORRIS

WHAT YOU NEED

Basic Pincushion Tool Kit (page 9)

Felted wool sweater (see Felting, page 17)

Sewing machine (optional)

Knitting needle

Embroidery floss, off-white

5 white buttons (1/4 inch)

18 inches thin coordinating ribbon

WHAT YOU DO

1 Make the pattern for the sweater using the template (page 119). Position the pattern at the bottom edge of the felted sweater, on the sweater hem or ribbing. Cut two pieces. Lay the pocket pattern at the neck edge of the sweater, and cut two pockets. Set the pockets aside.

2 Place the sweater pieces with right sides together and pin. Machine stitch or hand sew them with a 1/4-inch seam allowance, leaving the bottom edge open. Turn the sweater right side out, using a knitting needle to help push out the corners.

3 Stuff the sweater firmly with bits of polyester fiberfill, filling the sleeves first and working your way back to the opening. Hand stitch the bottom closed using a whipstitch with matching thread.

4 Stitch the pockets in place using a blanket stitch with embroidery floss and an embroidery needle. Sew a blanket stitch around the neck, the bottom of the sleeves, and down the center front, a little off center. Stitch the buttons in place down the front.

5 Thread the large-eye embroidery needle with coordinating ribbon, and stitch it in place at the neck. Tie a small bow.

Turtleneck Variation

Create this pincushion the same way you did the sweater pincushion, but place the turtleneck pattern at the neck edge of the sweater. Slide the pattern down so the top rests just below the ribbing or hem of the neck of the wool sweater. Follow the dotted lines of the pattern to cut the turtleneck straight up, through the finished neck edge of the wool sweater. Sew the turtleneck the same as for the sweater pincushion, except sew the bottom closed and leave the neck end open for stuffing. Stitch on buttons at the neck, if desired. (Omit the pockets for the turtleneck variation.)

fruitfulday

Almost too luscious to pierce with a pin, this pear, plus the apple and banana variations, makes a scrumptious centerpiece for a sewing basket——or fruit basket.

DESIGNER

JOAN K. MORRIS

Basic Pincushion Tool Kit (page 9)

1/8 yd. light green silk, 2 shades

Dark green silk scraps

9 x 12-inch felt

Sewing machine (optional)

Thread, black

Knitting needle

3-inch wood-covered wire

Wire cutter

Hot glue and glue gun

WHAT YOU DO

1 Create a pattern from the template (page 121) for the pear on scrap paper. Cut four pear panels, two of each shade of light green silk. Cut four rectangles of felt, at least 1/2 inch larger than the pear panels. Cut four leaves from the dark green silk scraps.

2 Layer each pear panel with a piece of felt on the wrong side of the silk. Using black thread, machine stitch or hand sew diagonally across the silk and felt, sewing parallel lines 3/4 inch apart. Begin and end each line of stitching on the exposed felt. Turn the fabric 90° and repeat, creating diamond shapes with the quilting lines.

3 Repeat step 2 for all of the pear panels.

4 Lay two of the stitched pear panels with right sides together. Stitch one side with a 1/4-inch seam allowance. Lay another panel in place, with right sides together, and stitch one side. Position the last pear panel and stitch it in place, leaving a gap in the seam, and a small space open at the top to fit the stem and leaves later.

5 Clip the curves (see Clipping Curves and Corners, page 15) and turn the pear right side out. Using small pieces of polyester fiberfill, tightly stuff the pear. Use the eraser end of the pencil to help move the stuffing into position in the pear and reach every corner. Hand stitch the opening on the side closed.

6 Place two of the leaf pieces with right sides together. Machine stitch or hand sew around the leaf with a 1/4-inch seam allowance, leaving the stem section unstitched. Turn the stitched leaf right side out and push the ends

out with the knitting needle. Machine stitch or hand sew veins onto the leaves.

7 Hot glue the leaves onto one end of the wood-covered wire, wrapping the leaf stems around the wire. Dab additional hot glue onto the end, and push it into the small hole at the top of the pear.

Silk Apple Variation

Use the apple template (page 121) to create a pattern, and cut the pieces from red silk. Follow steps 1 through 5 for the pear, except sew the quilting lines ½ inch apart. Then, after step 5, run a threaded needle from the center bottom of the apple to the center top of the apple, pulling tight to create a dimple in the bottom and the top. Knot the thread, and continue with steps 6 and 7 for the pear.

Silk Banana Variation

Use the banana template (page 121) to create a pattern, and cut the pieces from yellow silk.

Follow steps 1 through 3 for the pear. In step 4, start with banana panels A and B (with stems), and then add the last panel without a stem. Complete the banana following step 5 for the pear, omitting steps 6 and 7 for the leaves and wooden stem.

sewing with silk

Needles

Silk requires a sharp needle. Put a new needle on your sewing machine whenever starting a new project with silk. A dull needle can damage the fibers and create pulls or holes instead of piercing through them as a sharp needle will do.

Pins

Silk pins are super-sharp. Ball-point pins (for sewing knits) or just regular pins that are dull from use, can mutilate the fibers just like a dull needle will. Use either silk pins or the sharpest pins you have, and keep them in the seam allowance, rather than piercing the main fabric, to protect the look of the finished work.

Scissors

Be sure you use fabric-only scissors when cutting silk, and make sure they are sharp. Sharp scissors will keep the fabric from slipping as you cut. (See Scissors, page 9).

Oil

Don't oil your sewing machine before sewing with silk. Any oil residue will leave a permanent stain on the silk.

cute+curious

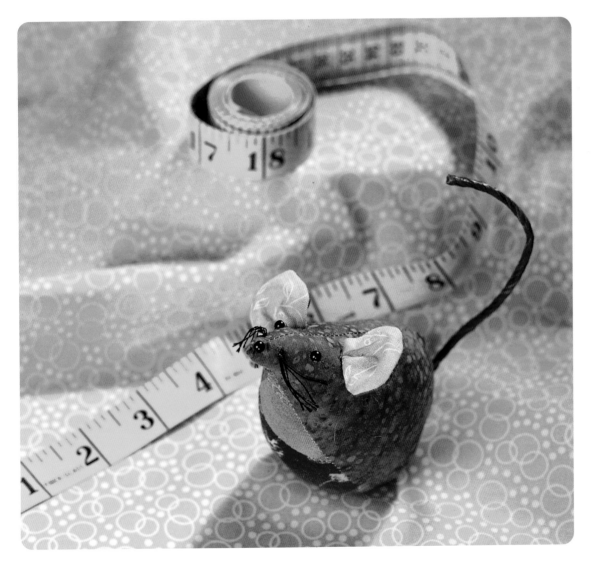

atch the cat when this little creature is out. Cuter than the real thing, he stays upright with a small river rock sewn inside for a base.

DESIGNER

JOAN K. MORRIS

WHAT YOU NEED

Basic Pincushion Tool Kit (page 9)

Assorted fabrics scraps, browns and pink

Sewing machine (optional)

Knitting needle

1-inch, flat, round river rock

Hot glue and glue gun

6-inch wood-covered wire

Embroidery floss, black

3 black seed beads

½"

WHAT YOU DO

1 Make a pattern from the template (page 122) for the mouse.

2 Piece together strips of pink and brown fabrics, sewing the strips with narrow seams, and pressing them open. Cut one chest out of the pieced fabric. Cut two body pieces from brown fabric, and cut two ears from brown and two ears from pink fabric.

3 With right sides together, machine stitch (or hand sew) the body pieces with a ¼-inch seam allowance. Sew from the tail area, up the back, and over the nose ½ inch, creating the point of the nose (see above).

4 Machine stitch or hand sew the chest piece in place, leaving an opening at the bottom large enough to fit the river rock. Clip curves in the seam allowance and turn the mouse right side out. Push out the points carefully with a knitting needle.

5 Stuff the body firmly with polyester fiberfill, a little at a time, starting at the nose. Use the knitting needle to push the stuffing into the nose point.

6 Insert the rock into the bottom of the body, and position it for the mouse to stand upright. Hot glue the rock in place.

7 Position the wood-covered wire for the tail, bend it into the desired curl, and glue it in place with hot glue. Then, close the hole at the bottom, hand stitching over the rock and the wire.

8 Place the brown and pink ear pieces with right sides together and stitch them, leaving an opening for turning. Turn them right side out, and hand stitch them in place on the mouse.

9 Hand stitch the seed beads in position for the eyes and the nose. Stitch black embroidery floss through the snout for the whiskers. Place a dot of fabric glue at the base of the whiskers to keep them in position, and separate the strands.

stardust

These lush velvet squares will add opulence to your sewing box. Dusted with golden stars, they're perfect for the girl who likes a little glitter.

DESIGNER

MARY-HEATHER COGAR

WHAT YOU NEED

Basic Pincushion Tool Kit (page 9)

Fabric chalk

Ruler Velvet, two contrasting colors

Thread, matching colors 10 gold seed beads

Metallic gold thread

Beading needle

Wool batting (optional)

Sewing machine

WHAT YOU DO

1 Using fabric chalk and a ruler, draw a 4³/₄-inch square on each color of velvet. Cut out the squares carefully using sharp scissors. Pin the pieces with right sides together.

2 Thread the sewing machine bobbin with the color of thread matching the bottom velvet, and thread the top of the machine with the color to match the top velvet. Stitch the pieces together with a ¹/₄-inch seam allowance. Leave a 1¹/₂-inch gap in the seam to turn the fabric.

3 Turn the fabric right side out, carefully pushing out the corners. Gently stuff with wool batting, and hand stitch the opening closed.

4 Thread the beading needle with metallic gold thread and sew 10 seed beads onto the top side of the pincushion. Thread an embroidery needle with metallic gold thread and embroider eight small lines around each seed bead for rays of light.

no tell-tail sign

If you tie a knot with this glittery thread, it will show. So leave the gleaming to the stars, and hide the tail of your thread. Start by bringing your needle through the pincushion from the bottom to the top, leaving a 2-inch tail at the bottom. When you're ready to cut the thread, pull gently on the tail, press on the pincushion, and snip close to the velvet. The tail will slip inside the pincushion when the fabric bounces back to form.

beesewing

beehive pincushion

WHAT YOU NEED

Basic Pincushion Tool Kit (page 9)

8 x 10-inch wool felt, gold

Wool felt scrap, dark brown

Embroidery floss, gold, bright gold, dark brown

WHAT YOU DO

1 Make a pattern from the template (page 122). Use the pattern to cut two hive pieces and one base from the gold felt. Cut one door from the dark brown felt.

2 Stitch the door to the bottom center of one of the hive pieces using small running stitches and two strands of dark brown floss.

3 Lay the hive pieces with wrong sides together. Using a whipstitch and three strands of gold floss, stitch them together along the sides, leaving the bottom open.

4 Thread and knot the needle with six long strands of dark brown floss (long enough to wrap around the hive five or six

The only things sweeter than this little hive for your sewing basket are the honeybee pins you make to go with it. You won't want to sew with ordinary pins again.

DESIGNER

CASSI GRIFFIN

times). Bring the threaded needle up through the inside of the hive and out near the top; leave a 2-inch tail inside the hive.

5 Repeat step 4 using four long strands of bright gold floss, bringing it out next to the brown floss. Leave the gold and brown strands hanging until step 7.

6 Stuff the hive lightly with polyester fiberfill to make embroidering easier—you'll add more stuffing later.

7 Using a couching stitch and the brown and bright gold threads, wrap and stitch around the hive five or six times. Space the brown wraps ½-inch apart and secure them with the gold thread. At the door, just slide the needle and thread behind the brown felt and continue stitching on the other side.

8 Whipstitch the base onto the hive using three strands of gold floss, leaving a 1½-inch opening to finish stuffing.

9 Stuff firmly until the pincushion is about three-quarters full. Finish stuffing with rice or lentils to give the cushion weight. Then sew up the gap.

TIP | BEE PRETTY

For an even prettier finish, leave the needle and thread hanging when you stop to stuff. After topping off with rice or lentils for weight, pick up the needle and continue whipstitching to close the gap.

bee
pins

WHAT YOU NEED

Clear shrink plastic

Straight pins

Bee paper punch

High-quality colored pencils, yellow, white, black

Thick rag or hot pad

Fine-grain sandpaper

Baking sheet

Oven

WHAT YOU DO

1 Rough the shrink plastic with fine-grain sandpaper to help the pencil color adhere in the next step.

2 Using the bee punch, make bees from the sanded plastic. Use the pencils to fill in the bees with color.

3 Put the bees colored side down on a thick rag or hot pad. Push a straight pin completely through the middle of one bee. Repeat for all bees.

4 Place the bees on a cookie sheet with the pin sticking straight up.

5 Shrink the bee pins in the oven according to the directions on the shrink plastic.

6 Remove them from the oven, and let them cool. Then swarm your hive with bees!

TIP
PINS OF A DIFFERENT COLOR
Choose a different theme for your pins—ladybugs, animals, or stars and moons—and follow the Bee Pins instructions to customize pins to every whim.

sunny-sideup

*Y*ou won't be scrambling for pins with these eggs on your plate. Add a side of bacon as a needle book, and you've got the perfect combo.

DESIGNER

JEN SEGREST

WHAT YOU NEED

Basic Pincushion Tool Kit (page 9)

Craft felt, camel tan, beige, rusty brown, white, yolk-yellow,

Craft thread, beige, white, golden yellow

bacon needle book

WHAT YOU DO

1 Cut two 7 x 2-inch pieces from camel tan felt for the front and back, and two $6\frac{3}{4}$ x $1\frac{3}{4}$-inch pieces from camel tan felt for the needle book pages. Also cut thin strips of beige and rusty brown for the bacon stripes.

2 Lay the needle book pages together and hand sew a blanket stitch around the edges with matching thread. Set aside.

3 Arrange the thin strips of browns and reds on top of the front piece to create the stripes on the bacon. Move and trim the strips as needed for the desired look.

4 Pin the strips down and hand sew a running stitch down the center of each strip with a matching thread. This stitch will secure the strips and also lend a bumpy bacon texture.

5 Lay the back piece and front piece wrong sides together, and hand sew them with a blanket stitch around the edges in matching thread, ending at a corner. Leave the thread attached.

6 Run the needle inside to the other corner. Create a bottom loop with the thread from one corner to the other—large enough to hold the book shut. Then knot off the thread in the last stitch, and lose the end inside of the bacon (see Losing the Thread, page 16).

7 Position the blanket-stitched needle book page from step 2 inside the folded bacon case. Attach it with a stitch at each corner of the fold, or with a blanket stitch where the bacon case and page meet.

TIP

THICK-CUT BACON

For a meatier bacon needle book, add more pages. Cut additional pairs of $6\frac{3}{4}$ x $1\frac{3}{4}$-inch pieces from camel tan felt. Blanket stitch the edges together, and sew them in with the other pages in step 7.

egg pincushion

WHAT YOU DO

1 Cut two 6-inch circles from white felt for the base. Pin them together and then carve away some of the edge for a more random, fried-egg shape.

2 Sew a running stitch in a 1½-inch circle in the center where the yolk will go.

3 Cut one 1¾- to 2-inch circle from yolk-yellow felt, and position it in the center of the white pinned base. Sew the outside edge of the yolk to the white base, with matching yellow thread in a very fine whipstitch or blanket stitch.

4 After stitching three-quarters of the way around, begin stuffing the yolk.

5 Continue sewing and stuffing as you go, using the eraser end of a pencil to pack the stuffing firmly. Finish the yolk edging.

TIP

INVISIBLE KNOT
A little twist to the loop in your blanket stitch will make a nearly invisible knot to hold your seam tight during stuffing.

6 Place small bits of polyester fiberfill between the layers of the egg base to add dimension. Sew a blanket stitch around the outside edge, adjusting or adding stuffing as you go. Then, knot the thread and lose the tail inside (see Losing the Thread, page 16).

Vegetarian Variation

If bacon isn't part of your sewing diet, skip that section and turn your sunny egg into its own needle book this way.

1 Cut a third and fourth layer of white felt to match the irregular egg shape from step 1 of the Egg Pincushion. Blanket stitch the edges together with white thread.

2 Position the egg yolk side down and lay the new base piece on the bottom of the egg, matching the curved edges exactly. Fold back half of the base felt, and pin it.

3 Blanket stitch the base to the egg along the fold line, using a small stitch so the base will easily unfold and lay flat. Store needles or long corsage pins on the inside pages of the needle book.

designsonfelt

Choose from four artistic designs or make your own on this nicely weighted felt pincushion.

DESIGNER

ELIZABETH HOOPER

cornflower cone appliqué

WHAT YOU NEED

Basic Pincushion Tool Kit (page 9)

Felt, cream, light and dark periwinkles, light and medium greens, white

Embroidery floss, coordinating colors

Basic Pincushion instructions (page 48)

WHAT YOU DO

1 Cut the following pieces from the felt:

Pincushion—one large semicircle in cream, two large circles in medium green, one semicircle band in medium green.

Appliqué—three flower B in light periwinkle, three flower A in dark periwinkle, three leaves in light green, three small circles in white.

2 Align the semicircle band along the curved edge of the large semicircle, overlapping the pieces by ¼ inch. Pin the pieces together, and hand sew along the edge with a running stitch to join them.

3 Using the photo as a guide, lay all of the appliqué pieces in place on the semicircle and adjust the overall composition as desired.

4 Set the other pieces aside and sew the leaves onto the large semicircle with a running stitch using light green thread.

5 Fold the semicircle in half with right sides together and sew a seam along the straight edge to form a cone. This will allow the appliquéd design in the next steps to overlap the seam.

6 Place the dark periwinkle flowers A on the leaves, and stitch them down using periwinkle thread.

7 Center a light periwinkle flower B and a small white circle on top of each of the dark periwinkle flowers and stitch around the small white circle using periwinkle thread. Stitch inside the periwinkle stitching with yellow thread.

8 Embellish the center with French knots using yellow and light green embroidery floss. Embellish the flowers with decorative stitches as shown using periwinkle thread.

9 Use the appliquéd cone top and remaining cut pieces to assemble the pincushion according to the instructions for Basic Pincushion (page 48), skipping step 2 for attaching the top piece to the side piece.

basic
pincushion

WHAT YOU NEED

Basic Pincushion Tool Kit (page 9)

Appliquéd top piece

Side piece

2 bottom pieces

Embroidery floss, coordinating colors

WHAT YOU DO

1 Choose the pincushion variation of your choice, and make a pattern from the template (pages 124-125) on scrap paper. Cut the pieces from felt according to the appliqué instructions for your variation. Then, follow the instructions for the appliqué—Blue Patchwork, Sunshine Bird, Purple Swirl, or Cornflower.

2 With the finished, appliquéd top piece, sew the long side piece in place on the wrong side of the top piece with a 1/8-inch exposed seam allowance. Set aside.

3 Create a pouch by sewing the two bottom pieces together with a 1/8-inch exposed seam allowance, leaving a 2-inch gap in the seam.

4 Pour 1/4 cup of rice or lentils into the pouch, and finish sewing around the edge to completely seal it. This will weight the bottom of the pincushion.

5 Sew the filled pouch to the side piece, easing the pieces together and adjusting them into alignment as you sew, leaving a 2-inch opening for stuffing.

6 Stuff the pincushion firmly with polyester fiberfill, using the eraser end of a pencil to push the stuffing into the corners as needed. Sew the opening closed.

blue
patchwork
appliqué

WHAT YOU NEED

Basic Pincushion Tool Kit (page 9)

Felt, white, navy blue, royal blue, Dutch blue, and light periwinkle

Embroidery floss, coordinating colors

Basic Pincushion instructions (left)

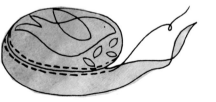

WHAT YOU DO

1 Create a pattern from the template (pages 124-125), and cut the following pieces from the felt:

Pincushion—One large square in white, two large squares and four side pieces in navy.

Appliqué—Four medium squares in navy; one small square and one medium rectangle in royal blue; one small square, one medium rectangle, and one small rectangle in light periwinkle; one small square, one medium rectangle and two small rectangles in Dutch blue; one small square, one medium rectangle, and one small rectangle in white.

2 Using the photo to the left as a guide, lay all of the pieces into place on the large white square and adjust the overall composition as desired.

3 Set the top pieces aside and stitch the four medium squares in navy onto the large white square using navy thread and a simple running stitch.

4 Place one set of top patches onto a navy square. Stitch each into place using matching threads. Repeat for all sets. Set aside.

5 Stitch the corner seams of the side pieces into one long piece with ⅛-inch exposed seam allowances.

6 Use the appliqued top and remaining cut pieces to assemble the pincushion according to the instructions for Basic Pincushion (page 48).

sunshine bird

appliqué

WHAT YOU NEED

Basic Pincushion Tool Kit (page 9)

Felt, yellow, light orange, brown, light green, and medium green

Embroidery floss, coordinating colors

Basic Pincushion instructions (page 48)

WHAT YOU DO

1 Cut the following pieces from the felt:

Pincushion—three large circles in medium green and one side band in medium green (cut on the fold).

Appliqué—one bird in yellow, one wing in light orange, one branch in brown, and seven leaves in light green.

2 Using the photograph as a guide, lay all of the appliqué pieces into place on one large circle and adjust the overall composition as desired. Make sure that the bird is positioned low enough to accommodate the branch and leaves.

3 Set the other pieces aside, and sew a running stitch around the bird using yellow embroidery floss.

4 Add the wing and stitch it in place with the same thread. Embroider alternating lines of yellow and orange in a simple running stitch on the wing, and add a French knot to the head for an eye.

5 Place the branch in an arc over the bird and stitch it in place using dark brown embroidery floss. Place the leaves and stitch them in place with light green embroidery floss.

6 Use the appliquéd top and remaining cut pieces to assemble the pincushion according to the instructions for Basic Pincushion (page 48).

purple swirl appliqué

WHAT YOU NEED

Basic Pincushion Tool Kit (page 9)

Felt, light periwinkle, purple, and lavender

Embroidery floss, coordinating colors

Basic Pincushion instructions (page 48)

WHAT YOU DO

1 Cut the following pieces from the felt:

Pincushion—one large circle in light periwinkle, two large circles in purple, one long side band in light periwinkle (cut on the fold).

Appliqué—one swirl in purple, 14 smaller circles of graduated sizes in lavender.

2 Using the photo as a guide, lay all of the appliqué pieces into place on the large light periwinkle circle and adjust the overall composition as desired.

3 Set the other pieces aside and sew the swirl onto the large circle in periwinkle with a running stitch using light periwinkle thread.

4 Position the graduated circles on the swirl and stitch using dark purple thread. Embellish the small circles with a French knot in dark purple thread as shown in the photo. Add French knots at the end of the swirl as well, if desired.

5 Use the appliquéd top and remaining cut pieces to assemble the pincushion according to the instructions for Basic Pincushion (page 48).

sweetdreams

This one's a softy—it features nostalgic fabric, a sweet and simple design, and a soothing scent, too.

DESIGNER

TONI WEBER

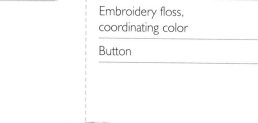

TIP   PINT-SIZE IT

For a smaller pincushion to tuck away in a tight space, start with a rectangle or square half this size.

WHAT YOU NEED

Basic Pincushion Tool Kit (page 9)

Fabric

Ruler

Fabric chalk

Sewing machine (optional)

Iron

Embroidery floss, coordinating color

Button

WHAT YOU DO

1. Using a ruler and fabric chalk, draw an 8 x 5½-inch rectangle directly onto your fabric. Double the fabric and cut two rectangles.

2. Pin the rectangles with wrong sides together, and sew a ¼-inch seam on all sides, leaving one narrow edge opening for turning. Clip the corners (see Clipping Curves and Corners, page 15), and turn the rectangle right-side out.

3. Tuck the open edges under, matching the rest of the seam, and press. Stuff the pincushion with polyester fiberfill. Be sure to pack the corners, but don't overstuff. Hand stitch the opening closed.

4 Thread a needle with a long strand of embroidery floss. Starting in the center of the bottom, poke the needle up through the center top and pull the floss through, leaving a 2-inch tail below. Hold the tail down, and wrap the floss around one side of the pillow. Bring the needle back to the bottom and push up though the center again. Give the floss a slight tug and wrap the next side (figure 1). Repeat for all sides to tuft the cushion.

5 With the needle at the center top, pass it through the button and back through the pincushion. Repeat again. Then knot the loose ends on the bottom of the pincushion and trim the excess. Tie the loose ends together in a knot and clip off the excess.

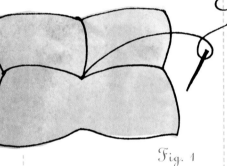

Fig. 1

TIP **STAB AND SNIFF**
As you're stuffing this cushion, add dried lavender or chamomile. Just make sure you include a top and bottom layer of polyester fiberfill. (And, if you've already stuck pins in, this isn't the place to lay your head down.)

With your careful hand embroidery, these pincushions will be heirlooms to pass down to the next generation of crafters and sewers.

DESIGNER

JEN SEGREST

WHAT YOU NEED

Basic Pincushion Tool Kit (page 9)

Craft felt, various bright colors

Craft thread, matching colors

2 felt buttons (page 56)

WHAT YOU DO

1 Cut two 3-inch circles from felt for the top and bottom of the pincushion. Cut a 2-inch-wide strip of felt long enough to go around the circle with a little overlap—about 9½ inches—for the side.

2 Hand sew the side to the top circle using a buttonhole stitch, overlapping the ends of the side toward the finish. Cut any excess length from the side.

3 Repeat step 2 to sew the side to the bottom, but stop three-quarters of the way around to begin stuffing.

4 Stuff very firmly with polyester fiberfill, being sure to stuff into the edges and corners. Then continue sewing to close the gap. Add more stuffing as you go, making the cushion as firm as possible.

5 Mark the center of the top and bottom of the cushion. Make a felt button (see sidebar, page 56), and thread a long needle with the thread hanging from the finished button. Push the needle into the top center mark and out the bottom center mark. Leave the thread hanging.

6 Repeat with a second button, starting from the bottom center and bringing the needle out on the top center, so a button is on each side and its thread is on the opposite side.

7 Insert the threaded needle back into the top center, under the button, and bring it out on the bottom center, under the other button. Pull both threads taut to tuft, or dimple, the pincushion on the top and bottom. Make a surgeon's knot to tie it off. Trim the thread.

Felt Button

Create two of these hand-worked buttons to use for the Timeless Treasure pincushion. You will need felt and a needle and thread in a matching color.

1 Cut a 1½- to 2-inch circle of felt. Thread a needle with a matching color of thread, knotting it.

2 Sew a running stitch around the outside edge of the circle for a drawstring. Draw the thread tightly shut, knot it, and then flatten the ball.

3 Run the threaded needle through the gathered center and out the folded edge, and sew another running stitch on the folded edge itself.

4 Draw tightly for a drawstring again, and press the gather into the middle as you pull the thread to close around it. Pull tight and run the thread to the opposite side. Pull again, and knot. Repeat several times to close up any gap. Leave the thread hanging to use to attach the button later.

9 At the end of each branch, make a three-spoke wheel of chain stitches in another color, and then whipstitch twice over the twig for a more finished look. Or, use a single chain stitch for a flower bud. Stitch felt flowers to the top and sides as well, if desired.

10 Fill in open areas with running vertical and horizontal stitches, beads, or flowers made with a chain stitch.

8 Embroider a branch around the side using a feather stitch. If desired, cut felt for flowers (see Petals, Leaves, Pompoms and More, page 57), and slide them onto the needle, knotting them into the embroidery as you go.

Leaves, Pompoms and More, page 57)

TIP CIRCLES FROM SQUARES

To improvise a 3-inch circle, cut a 3-inch square first. Then, just round the corners into a circle.

Petals, Leaves, Pompoms, and More

Clover Leaves

Cut a 2-inch square of felt and snip the center of each side, going one-third of the way in. Round three of the corners.

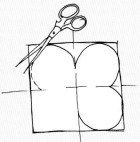

Flower Petals

Follow the instructions for Clover Leaves above, starting with a 1-inch square of colorful felt. Round all four corners into petals. Layer two colors of flowers to create violets, or use clumps of one color to make a hydrangea.

Circle Petals

Cut ½-inch circles of felt, folding them and placing them side-by-side for a full, ruffly flower. After attaching, clip into the petals at regular intervals for a geranium or marigold look.

Pompoms

Run a yellow thread in and out of the fabric where you will place a flower. Lay the thread open. Cut tiny "french fries" of felt in purples or pinks, placing lighter pieces toward the center. Lay them in a bunch between the open threads, and knot the thread around them tightly. Trim the long ends to even out the petals for a mum look.

Stamens

After attaching a flower with a looping stitch (as for a button), go back with a bright orange or yellow thread, pass through the center, and knot the thread. Trim it to the desired length for a colored stamen center.

Embroidered Vines

Use a feather stitch to sew a branch. At the end of each branch, stitch a three-spoke wheel of chain stitches in another color for flowers. Or, sew a single chain stitch for a flower bud.

sew nostalgic

A little flea market fabric here, a vintage button there—instant simpler times.

femininemystique

Lacy with vintage appeal, this pillow pincushion is all girl.

DESIGNER

JOAN K. MORRIS

WHAT YOU NEED

Basic Pincushion Tool Kit (page 9)

Fabric, green and green striped

Lace fabric or doily

1 yard silk cord

3 shell buttons, 1 inch, ¾ inch, 1¼ inches

1-inch button form

Iron

Sewing machine (optional)

WHAT YOU DO

1 Cut a 10 x 7-inch rectangle of each of the green fabric, green striped fabric, and lace. Lay the green fabric face up. Place the lace face up on top of it. Machine stitch or hand sew around the edges with a ¼-inch seam allowance.

2 Lay the green striped fabric over the lace with right sides together, and pin in place. Machine stitch or hand sew with a ½-inch seam allowance, leaving a 2-inch opening.

3 Turn the piece right side out, and stuff tightly with polyester fiberfill. Hand stitch the opening closed.

4 Thread the embroidery needle with the silk cord. Insert the needle through the center of the pincushion. Pull the cord through, leaving a 3-inch tail at the back. Loop the cord around one side of the pincushion and back to the bottom center. Go back through the pincushion to the top and repeat for each side. Pull the center tight, creating a tuft, and knot the ends of the cord together.

5 Cover the button form with green striped fabric, following the manufacturer's instructions. Sew it onto the pillow with a double-threaded needle.

6 Stack the shell buttons on the lace side of the pillow, and sew them in place through the holes.

elegantnotions

$\mathscr{E}$asier to do than it is to say, trapunto detailing adds dimension to this pincushion's base. Felt petals further embellish the Victorian-inspired design.

DESIGNER

RUTH SINGER

WHAT YOU NEED

Basic Pincushion Tool Kit (page 9)	Wool batting (optional)
Fine-weave silk douppioni	Felted wool or thick felt (see Felting, page 17)
Medium-weight cotton fabric	Decorative fabric
Cotton thread, coordinating color with the silk	Iron
Small pointed embroidery scissors	Steel pins to decorate
Tweezers	Sewing machine (optional)

WHAT YOU DO

1 Make a paper pattern from the template (page 123) or simply cut an 8-inch diameter circle. Cut one circle of douppioni and one of plain cotton. Press.

2 Trace circles from coins and spools in pencil on the right side of the cotton for the trapunto, following the markings on the template, or making your own design.

3 Pin the cotton and silk circles with wrong sides together. Using cotton thread, carefully hand sew a running stitch around each circle. Check the right side of the silk to make sure the stitches are neat and even for show.

TIP **ROOM IN THE ROUND**
Small circles will make your trapunting (bless you) harder than it has to be. Keep your circles moderately sized and away from seam allowances for the best effect.

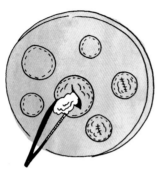

4 To stuff a circle, make a tiny, careful cut in the cotton with embroidery scissors. Don't cut the silk! Use tweezers to stuff tiny bits of stuffing into the circle, filling it evenly (see above). Use a whipstitch to sew up the slit. Repeat for each circle.

5 Create a pattern from the template (page 123) to cut 12 felted-wool edging shapes. Fold the finished trapunto circle in half and then quarters, and mark the folds with a tiny dot of pencil in the seam allowance.

6 Pin the felted shapes to the right side of the trapunto circle, facing inward. Match the straight edge of the felted shape to the outside edge of the circle. Use the quarter marks as a guide to space the shapes evenly. Baste them into place, and remove the pins.

7 To make the back of the pincushion, cut the paper pattern for the pincushion in half. Pin the half circles to the decorative fabric and cut, adding a 3/8-inch seam allowance along the straight edge.

8 Sew the straight edge of the semi-circles with right sides together, leaving a 2-inch opening in the center. Press the seam allowance open.

9 Sew the trapunto top and the bottom fabric, right sides together, with a 3/8-inch seam allowance. You may need to loosen the presser foot pressure if the felt is very thick. Remove the basting stitches. Trim the seam allowances by half and turn the pincushion right side out. Push the seams of the circle out neatly.

10 Stuff the pincushion, pushing the batting well into the curved seam, but don't overstuff or the pincushion will pucker. Hand stitch the opening closed.

11 Arrange steel pins around the circles in the cushion and according to the photo, or make your own design.

whipstitchitgood

Whip up this cupcake-shaped pincushion from scratch with a dash of scrap fabric, colorful stitching, and a few sweet buttons for a garnish.

DESIGNER

MEG ROOKS

WHAT YOU NEED

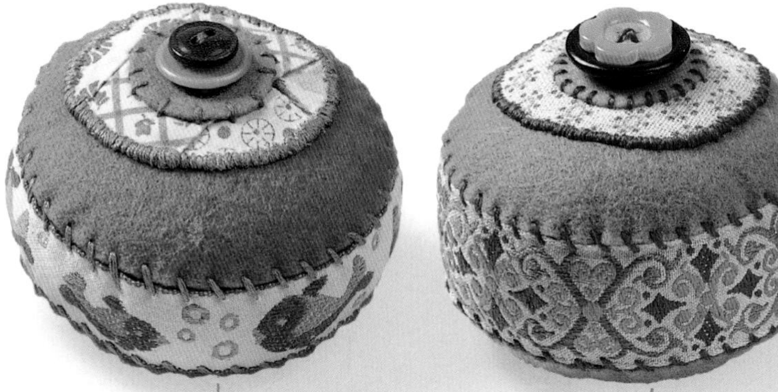

- Basic Pincushion Tool Kit (page 9)
- Wool felt, 2 colors (see Felting, page 17)
- Vintage fabric
- Embroidery floss
- Vintage buttons (large and small)
- Vintage trim, 1 inch wide

WHAT YOU DO

1 Cut two 3½-inch diameter circles from wool felt, one 2-inch circle of vintage fabric, and one 1-inch circle of coordinating wool felt.

2 Using embroidery floss, carefully hand stitch the 2-inch fabric circle to the center of one large felt circle with stitches side by side.

3 Using a wider stitch, hand sew the 1-inch felt circle on top of the vintage fabric. Then, sew the buttons in a stack on top.

4 Whipstitch the trim to the top felt circle. Sew the ends of the trim together, tucking under the raw edge. Then, whipstitch the bottom felt circle to the trim, leaving a 2-inch opening for stuffing.

5 Add the stuffing, filling with a layer of rice, a layer of polyester fiberfill, and another layer of rice. Pack it tightly, and whipstitch to close the gap.

twistedlids

This is your summer-camp craft project all grown-up with retro fabric and endless options for fun and funky trims from your local craft store.

DESIGNER

TERRY TAYLOR

WHAT YOU NEED

Basic Pincushion Tool Kit (page 9)

Standard canning lid and screw-on ring

Spray paint

2½- to 3-inch polystyrene foam balls

Serrated knife

Felt

Fabric

Decorative trims

Hot glue and glue gun

WHAT YOU DO

1 Spray the canning lid and matching ring with two to three coats of paint, following the paint manufacturer's recommendations for drying time between coats.

2 Use a serrated knife to cut the foam ball in half. Trim an additional ¼ inch from the bottom of one half-round.

3 Cut a 5-inch circle and a 3½-inch circle each of fabric and of felt.

4 Thread a needle with a long, doubled thread—make the thread as long as your reach. Knot the end of the thread, and use a ½-inch-long basting stitch to sew ¼ inch from the edge of a fabric circle. Leave the threaded needle attached, and set the circle aside. Repeat with a new needle and thread for the second fabric circle.

5 Drape the large felt circle over the smaller half-round foam shape. Trim the felt as needed to match the edge of the foam. (Neatness doesn't matter yet.) Make small cuts in the felt around the edge to smooth the felt to the ball. Glue the felt to the foam with hot glue.

6 Place the large fabric circle over the felt-covered foam, gently pulling the basting thread to gather the fabric. Stitch back and forth across the bottom of the shape to secure the fabric, like a spider web. (A messy one, at this point!)

7 Cover the jar lid with the smaller circle of felt, and attach with hot glue. Repeat step 6 to secure the small circle of fabric over the felt on the lid.

8 Put a few small dots of hot glue on the innermost edge of the ring. Slip the covered foam shape into the opening and gently push it into place. Hold it in place until the glue sets. Run some hot

glue around the inside of the ring as well, to further secure it. Hot glue the fabric-covered lid to the bottom of the foam.

9 Embellish the ring with funky decorative trims secured with hot glue.

TIP **UPSIZING**
For a larger pincushion, use a wide-mouth canning lid and a 5⅞-inch foam egg for this project.

Charming and girlish, this paper-doll dress pincushion will transport you back to childhood.

DESIGNER

NATHALIE MORNU

WHAT YOU NEED

Basic Pincushion Tool Kit (page 9)

Fabric, three prints, 1/4 yard each

Fusible interfacing (one-sided)

Iron and ironing board

Muslin, 1/4 yard

Sewing machine (optional)

String

WHAT YOU DO

1 Cut a 6 x 10-inch rectangle from the main fabric for the pincushion. Cut two 4-inch diameter circles from the second fabric for the top and base of the pincushion. Use this second fabric for the dress as well in step 2. Set the cut pieces aside.

2 Place the interfacing, adhesive side up, on an ironing board, and lay the remaining portion of the dress fabric, right side up, on top of it. Press with an iron to adhere them, according to the directions on the interfacing package.

3 Cut a 4 x 4-inch square of the third fabric, and repeat step 2 with the square.

4 Make a pattern from the template (page 120), and cut three of dress A from the main fabric with the interfacing backing. Cut three collar shapes, six cuffs, and three waistbands from the 4 x 4-inch square with the interfacing backing. Cut three of dress B from the muslin.

5 Pin each dress A onto a muslin dress B, leaving an even border of muslin all around.

6 Pin the dresses side by side and evenly spaced onto the rectangle cut in step 1. Keep them at least one inch from each end. Hand stitch the dresses in place, sewing close to the edge of dress A.

7 Pin the collars, cuffs, and waistbands to the dresses, and hand stitch them in place as well.

8 Pin the shorter edges of the rectangle, right sides together, and machine stitch, or hand sew, the seam. This is the body of the pincushion. Set aside.

TIP

USABLE FUSIBLE

Take care when using fusible interfacing so that your iron does not touch the adhesive side or it's goodbye shiny, smooth iron and hello burned, sticky mess. If your fabric does not completely cover the interfacing, cut the interfacing down to size to prevent any mishaps.

9 To make the piping, cut four 1½-inch-wide strips of the third fabric (used for the collar and cuffs) on the diagonal. Stitch pairs of the strips together along the narrow ends to make two strips that each measure longer than 10 inches. Fold each strip in half lengthwise, wrong sides together, and press along the fold with your fingers.

10 Cut two pieces of string 12 inches long, and stretch one inside the furrow of each folded strip. Machine or hand baste the strips closed.

11 With the body of the pincushion still inside out from step 8, pin a piping strip completely around the bottom edge on the right side, matching the raw edges.

12 Carefully open up the ends of the piping and clip the inside string to the exact length of the circumference of the pincushion. Close the piping back up, overlapping the ends and turning the outer end under, cutting off any excess. Baste the piping to the pincushion and remove the pins.

13 Repeat steps 11 and 12 with the other piece of piping, sewing it to the top edge of the pincushion.

14 Leaving the pincushion inside out, pin one of the fabric circles from step 2 to the bottom of the pincushion, right sides together. Baste in place and remove the pins.

15 Using a zipper foot, or hand sewing, stitch all the way around the bottom of the pincushion, stitching in the "ditch" of the piping—as close to the string as possible.

16 Repeat steps 14 and 15 to attach the top piece, leaving a 2-inch gap to turn the fabric right side out.

17 Turn the fabric right side out and stuff it firmly with polyester fiberfill, using the eraser end of a pencil to help work the stuffing into the corners. Hand stitch the opening closed.

TIP CUTTING ON THE DIAGONAL

To cut a piece on the diagonal, or on the "bias," cut at a 45° angle to the selvage edge. The cut piece will have more give and flexibility to wrap around corners and curves when used for piping. (Perhaps a metaphor for life for those who feel they're always going against the grain.)

kitchenstitchin'

*I*f Scarlett O can sew a dress from curtains, you can make a pincushion from potholders. Worry about how you'll get your hot brownies out of the oven tomorrow.

DESIGNER

TERRY TAYLOR

WHAT YOU NEED

Basic Pincushion Tool Kit (page 9)

2 pot holders

¼ yard fabric, coordinating color

Wool roving (optional)

Tapestry needle

Crochet thread, matching color

Buttons (optional)

WHAT YOU DO

1 Measure the dimensions of the pot holders, and add an inch to each dimension for seam allowances.

2 Cut out two pieces of fabric to the measurements determined in step 1. With right sides together, stitch three and a half sides of the fabric to create an inner pouch for the pincushion.

3 Turn the pillow right side out and stuff with wool roving or polyester fiberfill. Pack the stuffing tightly using the eraser end of a pencil to move it into the corners.

Leave the opening unstitched, and set the pouch aside.

4 With a hand-sewing needle and thread, baste the pot holders together, aligning the corners.

5 Thread the tapestry needle with a long strand (36 inches) of crochet thread. Start at one corner, leaving an 8-inch tail of thread, and sew together three sides with careful stitches. Continue around the corner onto the fourth side about ½ inch. Unthread the needle and re-thread it with the tail left at the start. Stitch around the first corner about ½ inch as well. Do not fasten off either side.

6 Slip the stuffed pouch into the stitched pot holders. Use the eraser end of the pencil to pack stuffing into the corners as firmly as possible. Stuff generously—the more stuffing, the denser and heavier the pincushion. Then whipstitch the pouch opening closed.

> **TIP** **SEAMS CLEVER**
>
> *If the pot holders are crocheted, as in this example, make your stitches match the crochet stitches for a virtually invisible seam. Or, if you are particularly clever, crochet the two pot holders together with a crochet hook using a slip stitch.*

7 Stitch closed the fourth side of the pot holders, using the tapestry needle and crochet thread hanging from the corner. Knot the ends of the thread tightly.

8 If desired, tuft the center of the pincushion by stitching at the center through all layers and pulling the thread tight to dimple, or tuft, each side, and knotting it securely (see Tufting, page 16). Add a decorative button if desired.

no-sewkitsch

These vintage adorables offer no-stitch kitsch in just minutes. They're a great use for wonderful old pieces that don't fit your style in the kitchen, but will be a charm in your sewing room.

DESIGNER

AMY KAROL

WHAT YOU NEED

Basic Pincushion Tool Kit (page 9)

Vintage teacup, eggcup, or small bowl

Glue stick

Decorative fabric

Vintage trims and notions

Hot glue and glue gun

WHAT YOU DO

1 Using your teacup as a guide, make a ball of polyester fiber-fill double the size of the cup opening. Wrap the fabric tightly around the ball of stuffing and test fit it in the teacup. It should fit snugly and fluff up at the top.

2 Remove the ball from the cup, and adjust the stuffing as necessary for a tight fit. Tie a long piece of thread around the ends of the fabric to cinch it together, as tying string to a balloon. Trim off the excess fabric.

3 Use a hot glue gun to line the inside and bottom of the cup with glue. Carefully place the fabric ball into the cup, pressing firmly, and let the glue cool and dry.

4 Using a glue stick, secure ribbon around the cup, if desired. Add trims and vintage buttons with pins on top.

Oblong Variation

If your vintage piece is rectangular, form the stuffing in step 1 into an oblong or tube shape. Then, wrap the fabric around the stuffing, like wrapping a present. Secure the fabric with hot glue, rather than thread. Then proceed with steps 3 and 4.

TIP GLASS CHOICES
Look for opaque glass vintage items to turn into pincushions. Opaque glass will mask the fabric, thread, and glue tucked inside.

creativeedge

WHAT YOU NEED

Basic Pincushion Tool Kit (page 9)

Vintage fabric, patterned

Felted wool or thick felt
(see Felting, page 17)

Sewing machine (optional)

Thread, coordinating color

Iron

Wool batting (optional)

WHAT YOU DO

1 Use the dragon scale template
(page 120) to create a pattern, or make your own pattern.
Cut 10 dragon scales from the felted wool. Cut one piece of fabric
5 x 3 $\frac{3}{8}$ inches and two pieces
3$\frac{3}{8}$ x 3$\frac{1}{8}$ inches.

Easy-to-use felt forms a modern silhouette around a funky vintage fabric base in these pincushions.

DESIGNER

RUTH SINGER

2 Pin the flat edge of the scales
around the edge of the large
rectangle, on the right side, with
the spikes pointing in. Leave a gap
at each corner. Baste in place, and
remove the pins.

3 Sew the two smaller pieces
of fabric together on the
long side with a $\frac{3}{8}$-inch seam
allowance, leaving a 1$\frac{1}{2}$-inch gap
in the middle of the seam for
stuffing. Press the seam
allowance open.

4 Lay the top and bottom
fabric right sides together,
and sew all sides with a $\frac{3}{8}$-inch
seam allowance. Remove the
basting stitches.

5 Turn the pincushion right
side out, and use a pencil
to gently push out the corners.
Fill with wool batting or other
stuffing, and hand sew the
opening closed.

offthecuffcreatures

They may be a little chubby, but no one could call these boys buttoned down. Sewn from repurposed shirt cuffs, they make the materials from old shirts as fun as when you first met.

DESIGNER

SUSAN MENTRAK

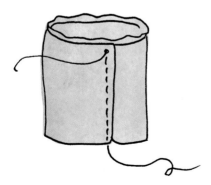

WHAT YOU NEED

Basic Pincushion Tool Kit (page 9)

Vintage shirt with cuffs

2 types of felt, regular weight and stiff

Drinking glass

Decorative ribbon

Embroidery floss, black and maroon

Vintage button (optional)

Assorted pins, flat head, corsage, or round head

Tiny pompoms

WHAT YOU DO

1. Cut a cuff from the shirt, trimming close to the seam. Button the cuff, and turn it inside out. Hand sew a running stitch along the closure edge of the cuff, being careful not to sew through to the front of the fabric.

2. Using a drinking glass sized to fit snugly into the cuff, trace circles onto both pieces of felt for cutting. Cut both circles. Set the stiff felt circle aside for the bottom piece.

Pin the regular felt circle to the raw edge of the cuff with the right sides together. Whipstitch the pinned pieces together.

Turn the cuff right side out and stuff tightly with the polyester fiberfill, till the cuff is about two-thirds full. Then, fill with rice or lentils to weight the bottom of the pincushion.

Fit the stiff felt circle into the bottom of the pincushion, over the rice or lentils. Hand-sew shut using a whipstitch.

Select a coordinating ribbon to decorate the seam along the top edge and hide the stitching. Sew in place with a whipstitch.

Thread the needle with black embroidery floss and knot it. Push the needle through the location for the eyes, letting the ends of the thread form the eyelashes. Sew parallel stitches to form the eye shape.

Keep the cuff button in place for the nose, or replace it with a vintage button. Shape a mouth with running stitches, using maroon embroidery floss and hiding the knot in the inside of the cuff.

TIP | **ALTER EGO**
Sew one face on the front of your pincushion and another on the back—then rotate your cushion daily to fit your mood.

Embellishing Pins

Make an eclectic array of embellished pins with buttons, beads, and baubles to top your pincushion, or even to use for sewing.

Jewels

Poke straight pins through pompoms and small beads, using permanent glue (cyanoacrylate) to keep them in place.

Flowers

Sew a small button to a larger button. Then glue beads to form flower petals around the smaller button. Stick a straight pin through the thread on the back, and glue the pin in place.

Buttons

Sew a small and a medium button together with a bead. Push a straight pin through the thread, and glue it in place.

Butterflies

Carefully glue the edges of two buttons for wings onto opposite side edges of another button for the body. Sew through the holes of all three buttons to secure them; then insert a flat-head pin through the thread in back, and glue in place.

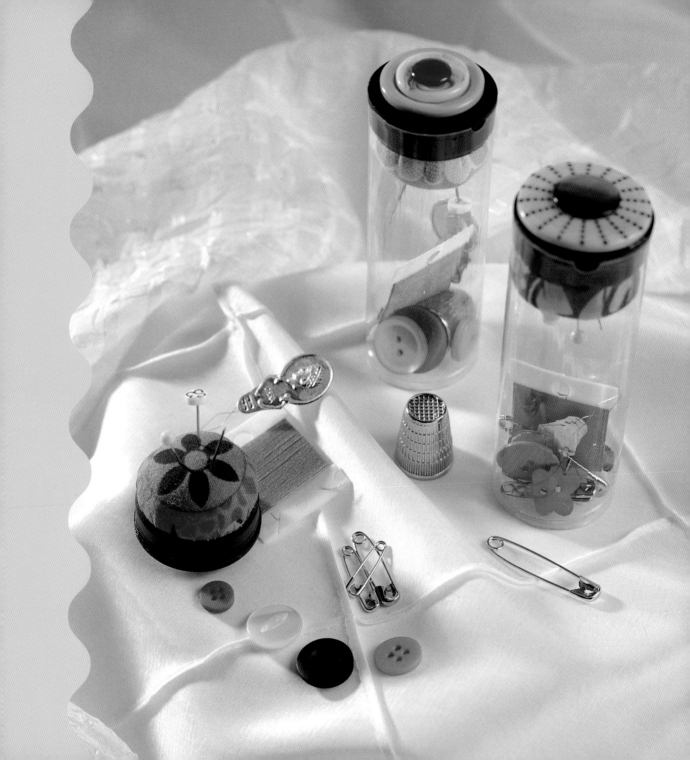

pretty & petite

When your sewing project calls for just a few
pins, reach for one of these cute mini-cushions.

*P*ins couldn't be closer when you need them than on this fabulous finger pincushion. It's a great gift for a crafter or sewer, too.

DESIGNER

JULIE ROMINE

WHAT YOU NEED

Basic Pincushion Tool Kit (page 9)

Lightweight cardboard

Scraps of coordinating cotton fabric

Sewing machine (optional)

Ribbon, rick-rack, or buttons

WHAT YOU DO

1 Make a pattern from the template (page 123) onto lightweight cardboard.

2 Lay the fabrics with right sides together, and trace lightly around the triangle with a pencil.

3 Sew before cutting the fabric, stitching directly on the line drawn. Make sure to backstitch at the start and finish, and leave a gap on the longest edge for turning the pincushion to the right side.

4 Cut around the sewn triangle, leaving a ¼-inch seam allowance. Clip the corners (see Clipping Curves and Corners, page 15), and turn right side out.

5 Stuff the side points lightly, using the eraser end of the pencil to help push the stuffing in. Stuff the main body firmly. Whipstitch the opening closed.

6 Overlap the outside points of the triangle, and hand stitch them together with a double-threaded needle for strength. Then stitch the center of a small length of ribbon onto the inside of the sewn points. Wrap the ribbon around, fold under the end, and stitch in place.

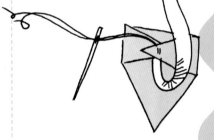

7 Be creative with rick-rack, ribbons, and buttons to embellish your finger pincushion.

sewonthego

This traveling kit can go where you go and serve you on the fly with a tube the perfect size for buttons, needles, thread, and a custom-made, pop-out pincushion.

DESIGNER

AMY ALBARRÁN

WHAT YOU NEED

Basic Pincushion Tool Kit (page 9)

Fabric

Bead storage tube with a 1³⁄₈-inch opening

Silicone craft glue

¹⁄₄-inch hole punch

Buttons or embellishments

Sewing notions

WHAT YOU DO

1 Cut a 3¹⁄₂-inch diameter circle of fabric, and hand sew a running stitch along the edge with a ¹⁄₄-inch seam allowance for a drawstring.

2 Pull both ends of the drawstring, gathering the fabric into a ball form. Stuff the sack firmly with polyester fiberfill. Draw the thread tight, and secure it with a knot to close.

3 Remove the cap from the bead storage tube, cutting off any plastic loop from the top of the cap. Dab silicone craft glue inside the cap, and spread it along the inside rim, staying clear of the edge.

4 Place the ball inside the cap, pressing it against the sides for a snug fit. Set a weight on top of the cushion for about 15 minutes to set the glue.

5 Use a ¹⁄₄-inch hole punch to clip two half-circle notches into the rim of the tube on opposite sides. This gives finger grip areas for popping off the cap.

6 Dress up your kit by gluing a stack of buttons, or other embellishments, on top of the cap. Just make sure they are flat so the pincushion can sit on its base when you're using it.

7 Let the glue cure overnight. Then, stash notions like safety pins, extra buttons, needle and thread, and even a thimble in your kit. You're ready to go!

spinthebottlecap

These mini-cushions are a new spin on recycling your bottle caps. Make a few extras to detail with your own twist.

DESIGNER

JEN SEGREST

bottle-cap pincushion base

WHAT YOU NEED

Basic Pincushion Tool Kit (page 9)

Craft felt, desired colors

Rolling cutter (optional)

Craft thread, matching colors

WHAT YOU DO

1 Choose felt colors for the top and bottom of the pincushion. Lay the bottle cap against a small square of the bottom color, and cut a circle the same size as the cap bottom. Round off any uneven edges. This is the bottom of the pincushion. Set aside.

TIP **COLOR SCHEMING**

Before making the base pincushion, check out the instructions for the variation you will make so you know the color scheme and any special instructions for the base.

2 Cut a strip of the bottom color of felt a bit wider than the height of the cap (¾ to 1 inch). Use the rolling cutter and guide, if needed. Wrap the strip around the circumference of the cap and cut it to length, allowing a slight overlap. This is the side piece for the pincushion.

3 Position the strip around the cap in a cuff with enough overhang on the bottom to create a place for the bottom circle of felt to fit. The cuff should overhang both the top and bottom of the cap slightly. Trim as needed.

4 Pierce the overlapping ends of the side piece with a needle and thread, from the wrong side of the felt, at the point the cuff hangs off the bottom of the cap.

5 Insert the bottom piece from step 1, laying it flush with the cuff edge. Whipstitch around the base, joining the bottom piece and the cuff.

6 After whipstitching the circle, tick the needle in and come out on one side of the cuff overlap. Sew a small horizontal whipstitch along the overlap to the top of the cuff. Bring the needle and thread to the outside near the edge. Leave the thread hanging to finish later. Set aside.

7 Cut a 3-inch-square piece of felt in the color for the top of the pincushion. With scissors, round off the corners into a circle.

8 Create a drawstring by sewing a running stitch around the outside edge of the circle, beginning and ending with the thread on the same side of the felt. Pull both ends of the drawstring, cinching the felt into a pouch. Twist the ends of the thread into a surgeon's knot to help in closing it later.

9 Stuff the pouch with polyester fiberfill to create a solid, hard ball. Draw the ball nearly shut and tie a knot. Work in a few more small bits of stuffing with the eraser end of a pencil. Clip the excess thread from the knot.

10 Remove the bottle cap from its felt sheath, and press the stuffed ball into the bottle

cap with the drawstring down. Squeeze the ball to fit it into the bottle cap, but make it as smooth as possible, without wrinkles. If the ball wrinkles or has folds, add more stuffing.

11 With the ball in place in the cap, work the cap back into the felt sheath, making sure the bottom felt is snug and flat against the cap.

12 With the thread remaining at the top of the cuff, use a small whipstitch, buttonhole stitch, or blanket stitch to sew the sheath to the ball, ticking the needle just into the felt to hold, not into the stuffing.

13 Decorate this pincushion with a chain stitch or add oodles of flowers or vine work (see page 57, Leaves, Petals, Pompoms and More). Or, make the Ladybug, Violet, Flower Basket, Mushroom, or Eye variations that follow.

ladybug bottlecap pincushion

WHAT YOU NEED

Basic Pincushion Tool Kit (page 9)

Bottle-Cap Pincushion Base (page 91) with a red ball and a black, brown, or green base

Craft felt, black, green, and flower colors (optional)

Craft thread, white or red

Cross-stitch thread, black

WHAT YOU DO

1 Cut a corner from a square of black felt about 1½ x ½ inch for the short, wide head of the ladybug. Use pins to hold the peak and sides of the ladybug head on the pincushion.

2 Sew around the perimeter of the beetle, where the ball and side meet. Bring a needle with unknotted thread in from one side, push it through the bottom corner of the head, and secure it to the lower edge of the pincushion ball with fine whipstitches (or a small running stitch).

3 Go in at the corner of the head, where you started, and run whipstitches up to the peak of

TIP STITCHING SPOTS

If cutting tiny circles of felt makes you see spots, dapple this ladybug by sewing a chain stitch in a circle with black thread for spots instead.

the head. Stitch across the back, marking the wing split. Then go back on the stitches just made with small couching stitches, returning to the peak of the head.

4 Stitch down the final side of the head with whipstitches, and then use a couching stitch over the perimeter of the beetle sewn in step 2.

5 Add two French knots for eyes with white or red thread, setting them 1/4 inch apart.

6 Add spots by sewing tiny circles of black felt in place with a whipstitch or running stitch.

7 To add antennae, pass a needle with unknotted thread in over one eye and out over the other. Then repeat, backstitching in and out of the same holes. Trim the thread to length.

8 Add flowers or leaves to the base of the ladybug pincushion, attaching them with a running stitch or chain stitch into the base felt.

violet bottlecap pincushion

WHAT YOU NEED

Basic Pincushion Tool Kit (page 9)

Bottle-Cap Pincushion Base (page 91) with dark brown felt

Craft thread, brown, dark green, flower colors, yellow

Craft felt, dark green and flower colors

WHAT YOU DO

1 As you make the Bottle-Cap Pincushion Base with dark brown felt, cut the side strip to about 1 1/4 inches wide, and sew the seam to close the side around the cap with the ball inside.

2 From the bottom, insert the needle behind the felt to the top edge of the bottle cap. Sew a line of backstitches just above the edge of the bottle cap. Fold down the excess on the cuff, covering the tack-down stitches and forming the lip of the pot.

3 Thread the needle with green thread and knot it. Hide the knot under the fold of the pot, and bring the needle up to the top center of the pincushion. Set aside.

4 Cut two four-leaf clovers from green felt for leaves. (See Petals, Leaves, Pompoms, and More, page 57). Insert the needle into the center of the larger clover leaf. Sew a running stitch around the inside center, being sure to space the stitches to come up on one side of a cut

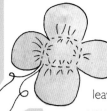

and down the other. Then pull the thread tight to rumple the leaves; shape them with your fingers.

5 Repeat with the second clover set at a 45° angle to the first. Bring the thread out at the top to one side of the center.

6 Cut flowers from various colors of felt. Fold one in half and attach it by passing the needle through it, about one-eighth of the way up from the fold. Repeat with the needle two more times. Set flowers at the points of an imaginary triangle, close together so they will press against each other, folding them in half to fit the next one in as necessary.

7 When done, shape and fluff the flowers with your fingers and scissors for the desired effect.

8 Add colored stamens to the flowers by stitching in and tying off yellow thread, or making French knots and leaving the trimmed tails sticking out.

flower basket bottlecap pincushion

WHAT YOU NEED

Basic Pincushion Tool Kit (page 9)

Bottle-Cap Pincushion Base (page 91) with brown ball and tan base

Craft thread, tan, green, flower colors

Felt, green, tan, flower colors

TIP **ATTACHING LEAVES AND FLOWERS**
Crowd leaves and flowers together as you attach them, so they will stand up and be full. Sew on a flower with a basic looping stitch, as if attaching a button.

WHAT YOU DO

1 Sew a row of vertical and horizontal stitches with tan thread around the tan side of the Bottle-Cap Pincushion Base to give the effect of a woven basket.

2 Embellish the top with small leaves at the edges or embroider trailing stems and flowers to the pot. Then add flowers to the top, packing them tight.

3 Cut a strip of tan felt for the handle so the handle is a finger-width taller than the basket. Round the ends of the strip, and sew a button hole stitch along the edges.

4 Attach the handle to the basket with a knotted thread, making a French knot on the outside of the handle to the base, and losing the thread inside (see Losing the Thread, page 16). The handle should be able to swing to the bottom of the pincushion as a finger strap for use while sewing.

death cap
mushroom
bottlecap
pincushion

WHAT YOU NEED

Basic Pincushion Tool Kit (page 9)

Bottle-Cap Pincushion Base (page 91) with a red ball and white base

Craft felt, white

Craft thread, white and brown

WHAT YOU DO

1 As you make the Bottle-Cap Pincushion Base with white felt, make the height of the outside band tall enough to fold inward and meet in the middle. Make the ball from a 3½-inch circle of red felt for the mushroom cap. Stuff it tightly, forming it to be full and flat rather than perfectly round.

2 Cut small circles of white felt and whipstitch them randomly to the top for spots, or use white thread worked in a chain stitch instead.

3 For gils on the underside of your mushroom, make a buttonhole stitch in brown with the spine at the outer underside edge and the descending stitches all the way back to the trunk.

Crimini Mushroom Variation

To make a crimini mushroom, replace tan for white and dark brown for red felts in the Death Cap Mushroom Variation.

eye bottlecap pincushion

WHAT YOU NEED

Basic Pincushion Tool Kit (page 9)

Bottle-Cap Pincushion Base
(page 91) with white felt

Craft felt, skin color
and eye color

Craft thread, white, black, skin
color, and coordinating eye color

Embroidery floss, eyelash color

WHAT YOU DO

1 Lay the base of the white pin-cushion against a small square of skin-colored felt, and cut a circle the same size as the bottom. Round off any uneven edges.

2 Cut a strip of skin-colored felt for a cuff, sized to hang ⅛ inch below the base and extend to the peak of the pincushion top. Make sure the ends of the strip overlap slightly when wrapped around the pincushion.

3 Begin sewing the cuff over the pincushion from the top of the overlap, using a small horizontal whipstitch. Be careful in the top half to sew only through the outer cuff, and not into the pincushion.

4 At the bottom, insert the round bottom felt, and whip-stitch it to the cuff with carefully spaced stitches.

5 Slide the needle back to the top, behind the cuff (being careful not to go through the ball), coming out $1/8$ inch from the top of the sewn side seam.

6 Take the needle over the edge and inside the cuff, and out the bottom. Before pulling the thread through, position the loop of thread to gather the top edge of the cuff and pull it down to form the corner of the eye. Pull the thread taut.

7 Reinsert the needle where it came out, and pass it through to the other side. Repeat steps 5 and 6 to create the other corner of the eye. Use a scissor tip to poke in the corners or shape the eye with your fingers.

8 Cut a $1/2$-inch circle of eye-color felt and a smaller one for the pupil from black. Position both in place on the eye; use straight pins to keep them in place.

9 Sew the pupil first, securing both the pupil and the iris to the ball. Bring the needle from the side and lose the tail inside the ball (see Losing the Thread, page 16). Sew small, evenly spaced stitches on the edge of the pupil with black thread.

10 Attach the iris in the same way, using coordinating thread. Make small stitches and space them about $1/8$ inch apart. Then, sew longer stitches between them to create the starburst look of an iris.

11 For eyelashes, use embroidery floss on the needle and come up from the side or bottom through the very corner of one of the eyelids. Sew a buttonhole stitch or blanket stitch along the eyelid edge. Place them closer together for thicker lashes.

12 At the corner of the lid, push the needle through the ball to the other eyelid and work that edge.

pincushion
or plushie?

The creatures in
this chapter are so
loveable, it almost
seems a shame to
stab them.

99

onpinsandneedles

*W*hat better place for all of your pins and needles than adding quills to this plushie little porcupine? He'll keep them to himself until you need one.

DESIGNER

AMY ALBARRÁN

WHAT YOU NEED

Basic Pincushion Tool Kit (page 9)

Furry fleece fabric, brown

Broadcloth, brown

Printed fabric, complementary color

Felt, light brown

Fabric chalk

Sewing machine (optional)

Thread, brown

Embroidery floss, black

WHAT YOU DO

1 Create a pattern from the template (page 123), and trace the pattern pieces onto the fabric as follows: two backs onto the furry fabric; two backs onto the brown broadcloth; two side heads, one center head, and two paws onto the light brown felt; one belly onto the dark brown broadcloth, one belly onto the printed fabric. Cut out the pieces.

2 Lay the two furry back pieces with right sides together. Sandwich them between the broadcloth back pieces. Pin all layers together, and machine sew, or hand stitch, the curved back seam with a ¼-inch seam allowance. Open the back, and lay it fur side up.

3 Position the belly pieces with wrong sides together, and lay them onto the sewn back with the printed belly fabric facing the furry back fabric. Using a small stitch for a tight seam, machine stitch or hand sew the belly and the back together with a ¼-inch seam allowance. Leave a 1½-inch gap at the neck for turning the layers right side out. Then, turn right side out.

4 The brown broadcloth on the inside of the body creates a pouch to hold the sand. Insert a small funnel through the opening into the pouch. Slowly pour sand until the pouch is almost full. Leave about $1/4$ to $1/2$ inch unfilled.

5 Fold the seam allowance under several times, and hand stitch it closed using a whipstitch. Sew tightly so the sand can't escape.

6 Stuff polyester fiberfill into the other pouch in the belly—between the printed fabric and the brown broadcloth. Use the eraser end of a pencil to evenly distribute it. For a plush and cuddly effect, don't overstuff. Fold in the seam allowance of the printed fabric, and blind stitch the seam closed. Set aside.

7 Sew a running stitch around the edge of a felt paw. Pull both ends of the thread, like a drawstring, to form a ball. Stuff the ball firmly with polyester fiberfill. Draw the thread tightly to close it, and tie a knot.

8 Use the thread from each drawstring to stitch porcupine fingers onto the paws. On the underside of the porcupine, blind stitch each paw in place.

9 Lay the side head pieces with right sides together. Using a backstitch, hand sew along side A from the neck to the snout, and around the point of the snout about $1/4$ inch.

10 Lay the chin piece onto side B of each side head, with right sides together. Sew one seam from the neck to snout on one side of the chin piece. Then sew the other seam from neck to snout as well, working the fabric and seam carefully to close the seam at the point the chin piece joins the snout of the head pieces.

11 Turn the head right side out, and stuff it firmly with polyester fiberfill.

12 Use a long strand of black embroidery floss to embroider a smile onto the snout and make a French knot for each eye. Add whiskers to the snout, if desired, with strands of floss.

13 Using the same floss, attach the little head onto the body with a running stitch, covering where the body opening was sewn closed.

TIP

CUTTING FURRY FABRIC

Don't give your porcupine a lopsided do; when cutting furry fabrics, cut with the backing facing you. Take careful strokes with the scissors to cut only the backing, not the nap, of the fur. When the backing is cut, clip through any strands of nap that are still holding the pieces together. That's the way to keep an even nap on your furry (or prickly) creature.

rulingtheroost

This funky chicken is cozier than the socks he came from and just as colorful.

DESIGNER

NATHALIE MORNU

WHAT YOU NEED

1 pair striped toe socks

Sewing machine (optional)

Felt

Thread, matching color

2 buttons

WHAT YOU DO

1 Slip one sock over the arm of the sewing machine, and sew a zigzag stitch along the line you want for the bottom of the chicken, or cut with pinking shears. Cut off the calf of the sock, snipping near the sewn line. If you are hand sewing this project, simply cut the sock along the line for the chicken with pinking shears to help prevent raveling. Then, cut the calf open down the side, and set aside for step 3.

2 Place the foot of the sock upright on a piece of paper, with toes facing up. Spread the opening into an oval shape. Pin it to the paper, and trace the outline of the opening. Remove the pins, and set the foot aside. Cut out the oval pattern with craft scissors.

3 Pin the oval pattern from step 2 to the fabric of the sock calf from step 1. Without cutting, sew a zigzag stitch just outside the paper oval. Remove the pins, and cut close to the stitching.

4 Turn the foot piece inside out. Pin the oval to the foot and sew all the way around with a $1/2$-inch seam allowance. Leave a 2-inch opening in the seam for stuffing.

5 Turn the fabric right side out, and fill with polyester fiberfill. Pin the opening shut, if desired, but don't stitch it yet.

6 For the wattle, turn the second sock inside out, toes and all. You will use the two smallest toes. Stitch a line between the third and fourth toes $1/2$ inches long. Trim as shown below.

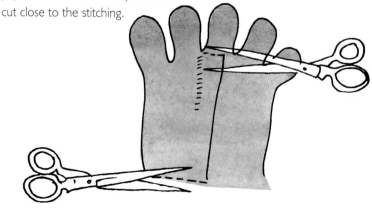

7 Turn the wattle right side out and lightly stuff just the tips of the toes. Turn the open edge inside and stitch the wattle closed. Hand sew the wattle to one side of the sock. Tack the fork of the wattle to the sock so it doesn't stick straight out.

8 Double-thread a needle, and knot the thread. Run the needle from one side edge of the sock to the other, inserting it below the big toe and coming out below the little toe. Pull the thread slightly to make little dimples in the sides, causing the toes to spread (see below).

TIP **CUT IT CLOSE**

All of the zigzag stitching in this project is not only fun, but also practical because it keeps the knit sock material from unraveling. So cut it close, but don't snip into a stitch—it keeps your raw edge intact.

9 For the beak, cut a strip of felt 1¾ x 4 inches. Fold it in half lengthwise and machine stitch or hand sew right next to the fold. Make a pattern of a beak, cut it out, and pin it to the felt, matching fold lines. Cut out the beak, and hand stitch it to the face above the wattle. Then sew on the button eyes.

10 Pat the stuffing in place, adding more if necessary. Stitch the opening closed.

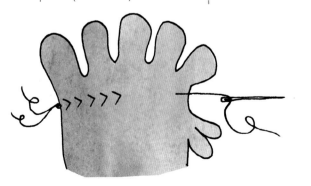

pinpals

You'll love pushing your pins into these plump little succulents. Watch out that they don't poke back!

DESIGNER

TONI WEBER

boycactus

WHAT YOU NEED

Basic Pincushion Tool Kit (page 9)

Green fleece or wool

Sewing machine (optional)

2 small buttons

1 small bead

Embroidery floss, brown

WHAT YOU DO

1 Make a pattern for the boy on scrap paper from the template (page 126). Cut out two body pieces, one gusset, one bottom, and four arm pieces from the fleece.

2 Sew one arm by laying two arm pieces with wrong sides together and stitching them with a 1/4-inch exposed seam. Repeat for the second arm. Pin the arms to the wrong side of one body piece, facing inward, positioned at different heights (like a cactus).

3 Pin the gusset to the same side of the body as the arms. Use pins liberally, and ease the fabric into the curve.

4 Sew a 1/4-inch seam around the cactus. Snip the top curve of the seam allowance (see Clipping Curves, page 15). Repeat, sewing the second body piece to the other side of the gusset.

5 Pin the bottom piece to the body. Sew with a 1/4-inch seam allowance, leaving a gap in the seam for turning right side out.

6 Turn the body right side out, and stuff with polyester fiberfill about three-quarters full, giving the body a nice firm feel. Add 1/4 cup of rice for bottom weight. Top off with more polyester fiberfill, and hand stitch the opening closed.

7 Use a pen to mark the placement for the eyes and nose. Sew on two small buttons for the eyes and a small bead for the nose. Embroider a simple mouth.

8 For the cactus spines, use a needle threaded with a long length of brown embroidery floss. Take the needle in and out at the top of the head, leaving a 2-inch tail of floss, and snipping off 2 inches on the other side. Continue in a random pattern across the head. Tie off and knot each spine, trimming as desired.

girlcactus

WHAT YOU NEED

Basic Pincushion Tool Kit (page 9)

Green fleece or wool

Sewing machine (optional)

2 small buttons

1 small bead

Embroidery floss, brown

⅝-inch pink velvet ribbon

Fabric glue

WHAT YOU DO

1 Make a pattern for the girl cactus on scrap paper from the template (page 126). Cut out two body pieces, one gusset, and one bottom from the fleece.

2 Follow steps 3 through 7 for Pin Pals, omitting the arms.

3 Cut a 10¾-inch length of ribbon, and sew a long running stitch down the center with matching embroidery floss.

TIP **CACTUS SOFT TOY**
To make a soft toy rather than a pincushion, leave out the rice when stuffing. Then embroider the face onto the cactus instead of using buttons, which could create a choking hazard for children.

TIP **REPURPOSING WOOL**
Scavenge material from an old fleece or wool blanket, or pick one up at a thrift store for the material for this project.

4 Cinch the ribbon into little folds along the floss for a blossom. Keeping the blossom pinched together, tie a knot in the floss at the bottom of the blossom to secure it.

5 Stitch the blossom to the side of the head with one of the loose ends of floss. Knot and snip the excess floss. Add a drop of fabric glue beneath each side of the blossom for extra hold.

tropicalsplash

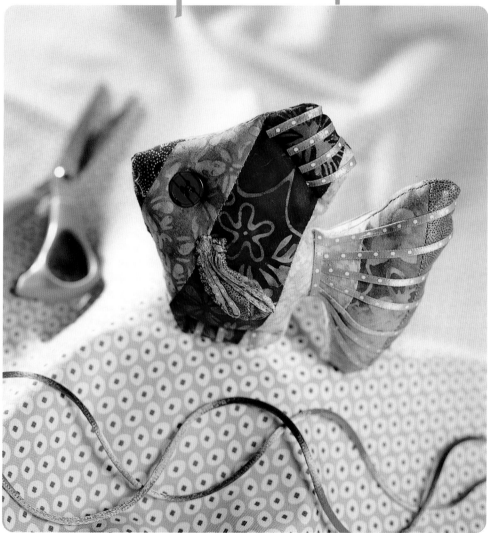

Hook up with this fishy (and companion kitty) and your pins will always be on deck.

DESIGNER

JOAN K. MORRIS

tropicalfish

WHAT YOU NEED

Basic Pincushion Tool Kit (page 9)

Printed fabrics, blues, greens, and purples

3 yards of $1/8$-inch green ribbon

2 purple buttons, $1/2$-inch

Iron and ironing board

Sewing machine (optional)

Knitting needle

Fabric glue

WHAT YOU DO

1 Create a pattern from the template (page 122). Cut strips of fabric 1 to 2 inches wide x 18 inches long. Arrange the strips with contrasting patterns and colors together.

2 Machine stitch or hand sew the long edges of the strips, right sides together, with a $1/4$-inch seam allowance. Fold the sewn piece in half with right sides together.

3 Pin the pattern to the fabric so the stripes run vertically on the fish (see below), and cut out two pieces at once.

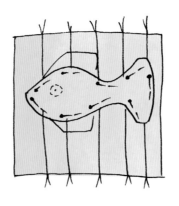

4 Machine stitch or hand sew the pieces together with a $1/4$-inch seam allowance, leaving a 2-inch opening on the lower front of the fish. Clips the seam allowance on the curves (see Clipping Curves and Corners, page 15).

5 Turn the fish right side out, using a pencil or knitting needle to push out the corners. Then, stuff it to the gills, using small bits of polyester fiberfill, starting with the back fin and working back to the opening. Hand stitch the opening closed.

6 Stitch between the body and each fin by hand or with a machine.

7 Cut out two fins from the left-over strips of fabric. Place them right sides together and stitch with a $1/4$-inch seam allowance. Leave open a small section for turning right side out. Clip the

tropicalcat

WHAT YOU NEED

4 blue buttons, $\frac{1}{2}$ inch

Fabric, assorted pinks and browns

Embroidery floss, black

1 yard of $\frac{1}{2}$-inch pink ribbon

WHAT YOU DO

1. Follow steps 1 through 5 for Tropical Splash, using the cat template and placing the pattern on horizontal stripes.

2. Stitch across the base of the ears; then hand stitch a pink bow to the cat's chin. Tack down the tails of the bow along the bottom of the head, creating a ribbon ripple.

3. Hand stitch buttons for the eyes, pulling tight to tuft the buttons (see Tufting, page 16).

4. For the nose, sew a satin stitch with embroidery floss; and for the mouth, sew a running stitch. For the whiskers, run the floss through from one side of the face to the other, cutting to length. Use fabric glue to keep them in place, and run glue down the whiskers as well to keep the floss together.

curves. Turn the fin right side out. Machine stitch or hand sew the opening closed. Stitch strips of green ribbon in place on the fin.

8. Hand stitch the eyes by running the thread through the fish from button to button, pulling tight to tuft the buttons (see Tufting, page 16). Create stripes on the tail and the fins with ribbon dabbed in fabric glue.

9. Hand stitch the fin into position, tacking it down across the narrow end and bottom of the fin.

feelingneedled

Not ready to forgive and forget? Maybe this guy is who you're looking for...

DESIGNER

JOAN K. MORRIS

WHAT YOU NEED

Basic Pincushion Tool Kit (page 9)

Felt, gray and white

Sewing machine (optional)

Black thread

Embroidery floss, black and red

WHAT YOU DO

1 Create patterns from the templates (page 127). Cut two top pieces from white felt and two bottom pieces from gray felt.

2 Machine stitch each white top to a bottom gray across the waist. With wrong sides together, machine stitch around the figure with a ⅛-inch exposed seam allowance. Start and end at the head, leaving the top open for stuffing.

3 Stuff the figure tightly with polyester fiberfill, starting at the feet and working toward the head. Machine stitch the opening closed.

4 With black embroidery floss, whipstitch hair on the head. Stitch an X for the eyes and a line for the mouth. Use a short running stitch for the hands, center circle, and shoe laces. Sew red embroidery floss in a satin stitch for the heart.

Woman Variation
Using the woman pattern, follow the same instructions as for the man. Change the lips to red, add more hair, and sew french knots for the necklace and bracelet. Use a buttonhole stitch for the dress hem, and a detached chain stitch for the flower

pinningzoo

*S*oft, charming, and simple, these embroidered, line-drawn animals are a great addition to a basic sewing kit. Without pins, they'd make an adorable accent for a baby's nursery.

DESIGNER

CASSI GRIFFIN

WHAT YOU NEED

Basic Pincushion Tool Kit (page 9)

Muslin

Water soluble marker or pencil

Embroidery hoop

Embroidery floss, various colors

Twill tape, natural color

Sewing machine (optional)

Iron

WHAT YOU DO

1 Draw or trace one of the template designs (page 127), or a design of your own, for embroidering onto the muslin with a water-soluble marker or pencil. Make sure the design falls within a 4 x 6-inch area.

2 Using an embroidery hoop and embroidery needle, embroider the design using one or two colors of floss and a simple outline stitch, backstitch, or stem stitch.

3 Measure a 4 x 6-inch section of the muslin, centered on the embroidered work. Cut it out, and also cut one plain 4 x 6-inch piece of muslin for the back.

4 Fold the twill tape in half with its ends matching. Pin it to the right side of the back piece at the top center. Match the ends of the tape to the raw edges of the muslin. The loop will be sandwiched between the front and back pieces when you sew.

5 With right sides facing, pin the front and back pieces together, and sew all around with a ½-inch seam allowance. Leave a 1½-inch opening at the bottom for stuffing.

6 Before turning the fabric right side out, press back the unsewn seam on the seam line to make hand sewing easier later.

7 Turn the fabric right side out. Use the eraser end of a pencil, or another tool, to push out the corners. Press the fabric, keeping the unsewn seam folded inside.

8 Stuff the fabric firmly with polyester fiberfill. Use the eraser end of the pencil to move stuffing into the corners.

9 Hand sew the opening closed, following the pressed edge of the seam line, and losing the thread inside (see Losing the Thread, page 16).

TIP GENTLE STUFFING
Stuff the pincushion firmly, but don't overstuff or the seams may buckle.

Designers

AMY ALBARRÁN was born and raised in Houston but now calls Austin, Texas, home. She shares her home with her Shih Tzu, Penny Lane, and an endless supply of imagination and craft supplies. Her works are the product of her creative inner child and her love for crafting. Amy was born into a family of artisans and finds joy in sewing, calligraphy, stamping, watercolors, and collecting. She creates sewn art based on vintage patterns and nostalgic children's craft books. Her works are created using mostly felt, vintage fabrics, and her grandmother's button collection. She shares her love of all things handmade on her blog, SewcialButterfly.com blog, which include a photostream on Flickr.com and an online shop at Etsy.com.

ANGELA BATE lives in the country where she, her husband, and their three small children enjoy the simple comforts of home. A long-time crafter and sewer, Angela sews, hunts for vintage treasures, peruses yard sales, quilts, reads, and enjoys her children in her spare time. Her inspiration comes from cottage, vintage, and shabby-chic design. She aspires to own a store where she can sell her creations and be surrounded by the fabric and books she loves. Til then, her online location is www.norththreads.com. She's also a featured artist at www.glitterandgrunge.com.

MARY-HEATHER COGAR is a CalArts graduate living in Los Angeles, where she constantly wishes for more rainy days. Her work is featured in several craft books, including *Greetings from Knit Cafe*, the *Crochet Pattern A Day Calendar*, and *Boho Baby*. She has taught creativity through cooking, art, music, yoga, dance, and theatre to children ranging in ages from 12 months to 12 years old. She has written and directed for children's theatre groups and developed the theatre program for a popular summer arts camp in Los Angeles. She sews, knits, crochets, spins yarn, embroiders, designs and sells her handmade creations and patterns, and blogs about it all at www.rainydaygoods.com.

CASSI GRIFFIN lives in the mountains of central Idaho with her three children. They picnic at the lake in the summertime, play in the snow in the winter, and care for their many furry and feathered pets year-round. She learned tatting and crocheting from her grandmother, sold home-made puppet kits door-to-door when she was eight, and her main craft pursuits now are needlework, crochet, and paper crafts. In the busyness of working part-time and home-schooling her kids as a single mom, Cassi re-energizes herself in the quiet respite of crafting. She finds her inspiration in the change of seasons and landscapes around her. Visual influences in her work include flower gardens, children's book illustrations, vintage fabric, Japanese design, historical films, and tag sales. Find her online at belladia.typepad.com.

ELIZABETH HOOPER started making pincushions while trying to come up with a creative, useful gift for her quilter sister. As she received positive feedback for her designs, her love for the pincushion form took off. Before she knew it, her home was overrun with them, and she started selling her work online. Elizabeth has been crafting since childhood and her repertoire of skills includes sewing, knitting, embroidery, painting, and photography. Visit her shop at loosestring.etsy.com and her crafting blog at squeakywheel.motime.com.

AMY KAROL grew up around quilters, writers, and creative eccentrics and considers herself very lucky for it (with a lot of funny stories to boot). She has a degree in Interior Architecture from the University of Oregon, and her paintings and monoprints have been represented by several Seattle galleries. Over 20 of her pieces are in a permanent collection in Japan.

Her textile art is strongly influenced by her love of needlework and quilt-making. Her large wall quilts and small framed art quilts show around the U.S. in various shops and galleries. Her new book *Bend the Rules*, is a sewing book geared toward beginners. She has also contributed to *The Crafter's Companion*, and *Simple Contemporary Quilts* (Lark Books, 2007). Her work has been featured in *Bust* magazine and the *Washington Post*. She is up to no good on a daily basis at her craft blog, www.angrychicken.typepad.com. She also has an art blog, www.kingpod.com, and an apron blog, angrychicken.typepad.com/tieoneon.

SUSAN MENTRAK graduated from the Columbus College of Art and Design. She has worked as a sculptor, a greeting card copywriter, a job coach for special education students, a bingo caller, a ministry coordinator, a retail manager, and a wedding coordinator, among other things. Her little cottage business, Joybucket

Design, was born in 2002 when the first doll she made sold within hours online. She has been producing unique, one-of-a-kind dolls and other creations ever since. Susan uses recycled, repurposed, thrifted, or donated materials in her crafts in order to be a good steward of our resources and environment. See her work online at www.joybucket.org or in specialty gift shops around the U.S. and Canada.

NATHALIE MORNU works as an editor at Lark Books, where one of her favorite tasks is making indexes. Occasionally she garners opportunities to dabble in a variety of crafts by designing projects for books. Some of those include: *Decorating Your First Apartment* (2003), *Making Gingerbread Houses* (2004), *Creative Scarecrows* (2005), *Creative Stitching on Paper* (2006), and *Fun & Fabulous Curtains to Sew* (2006). She also co-authored *Contemporary Bead & Wire Jewelry* (2005).

JOAN K. MORRIS'S artistic endeavors have led her down many successful creative paths, including costume design for motion pictures and ceramics. She has contributed projects to numerous Lark books, including *Beautiful Ribbon Crafts*, *Gifts For Baby*, *Hardware Style*, *Hip Handbags*, and many more.

JULIE ROMINE lives on a small ranch in Kansas with her husband, two young boys, and an assortment of pets. As a stay-at-home mom, she spends most days caring for and teaching her little ones. Whenever time permits, she draws patterns from the ideas that swirl in her head and makes her creations come to life. Julie learned to sew from her mother, who used to sell their creations to co-workers and at craft shows. She enjoys all kinds of crafting, from sculpting polymer clay fairies to hand embroidering onesies, but her favorite pasttime is sewing and inventing new things. Find her crafts online at www.blueberrymama.etsy.com or visit her blog at www.blueberrymama.blogspot.com.

MEG ROOKS is a once-and-future librarian and crafter from Portland, Maine. She is a big fan of decoupage, sewing, knitting, rug-hooking, glue-gunning, yard-saling, web-surfing, movie-watching, cookie-baking, etsy-shopping, re-cycling, you-tubing, book-reading, magazine-perusing, road-tripping, beach-combing, and picture-taking. She is very nostalgic and loves vintage children's books, fabric, and buttons, and she incorporates them in most of her crafts. Shop her crafty wares online at pixiegenne.etsy.com or find her blog at pixiegenne.typepad.com.

JEN SEGREST is a professional web designer who likes to reenact the Middle Ages on weekends as part of the Society for Creative Anachronism, where she specializes in and researches beadwork of the 11th to 14th centuries of the Germanic regions. Her want for cheap little thank-you gifts for other modern medieval artisans led her to develop her own tiny, and extremely handy, pincushions. Jen is, appropriately enough, middle-aged herself, and married to a computer geek. She has three dogs and two cats whose hair can always be found on her pincushions.

RUTH SINGER is a self-taught textile designer based in the U.K. She specializes in hand-constructed fabrics using traditional techniques from historical costumes and textiles. Ruth worked in museum education for several years and now pursues her creative business full-time. She has shown her work widely in the U.K. and in 2006 was selected as one of the best emerging makers by the British Crafts Council for Springboard at Origin, a major craft show. Ruth teaches textile history and practical techniques including handbag-making and fabric manipulation throughout Britain. Find her online at www.ruthsinger.com.

TERRY TAYLOR is a versatile project coordinator and editor at Lark Books. He is a prolific designer and exhibiting artist, working in media from metals and jewelry to paper crafts and mosaics. Terry has written several books for Lark, including *Altered Art* (2004), *Artful Eggs* (2004), *and The Weekend Crafter: Paper Crafting* (2002). He is co-author of Lark's well-received children's series: *The Book of Wizard Crafts* (2001), *The Book of Wizard Parties* (2002), and *Wizard Magic* (2003). At last count, Terry's project designs have been published in more than 60 Lark books.

TONI WEBER developed a life-long love of handmade things from her earliest creative memory of standing by her mother's side watching her sew a Cinderella costume. Toni's daily desire is to live a creative life, ranging from the extravagant—such as designing and sewing her son and daughter-in-law's wedding quilt—to the simplest act of adding a pretty garnish to a meal. She enjoys a wide variety of creative pursuits, but her first creative love is fabric and sewing. Her inspiration comes from nature, her children, and the everyday scenes of life—a row of pretty old homes on a tree-lined street or the way the color of her clothes hanging in the closet blend together. She lives on the Central Coast of California with her husband, children, and their very large kitty Otter. Find Toni's blog at simplesparrow.typepad.com, or shop for her crafts at www.etsy.com/shop.php?user_id=9160.

Acknowledgments

Thanks to everyone who contributed to this book and to all of the talented and creative independent crafters and designers out there today. Without their passion and sense of play, this book would not exist. Susan sends thanks across the continent to her mom and dad for fostering her creative abandon in those young, impressionable years. And for that great sewing machine and all of the fabric. She thanks Grandma Jo for the glorious larger-than-life dolls she sewed when Susan was a tyke, which brought much joy and instilled thankfulness for handcrafted keepsakes.

blossomneedle book

page 26

Enlarge 200% or size as desired

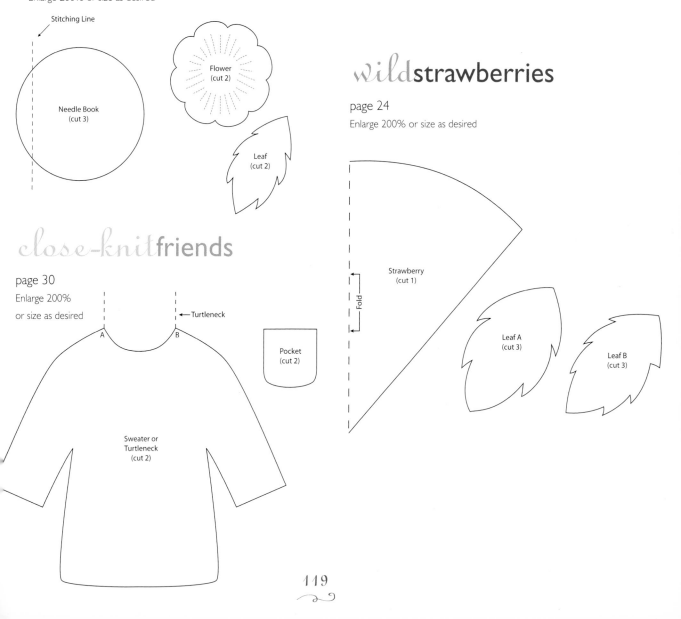

Stitching Line

Needle Book
(cut 3)

Flower
(cut 2)

Leaf
(cut 2)

wildstrawberries

page 24

Enlarge 200% or size as desired

Strawberry
(cut 1)

Fold

Leaf A
(cut 3)

Leaf B
(cut 3)

close-knitfriends

page 30

Enlarge 200%
or size as desired

Turtleneck

A   B

Pocket
(cut 2)

Sweater or
Turtleneck
(cut 2)

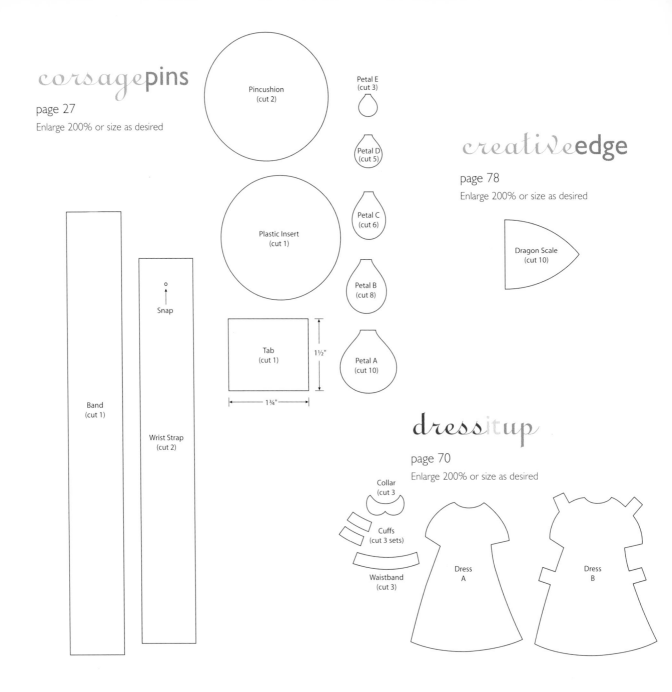

corsagepins

page 27

Enlarge 200% or size as desired

Pincushion
(cut 2)

Plastic Insert
(cut 1)

Band
(cut 1)

Snap

Wrist Strap
(cut 2)

Tab
(cut 1)

1½"

1¾"

Petal E
(cut 3)

Petal D
(cut 5)

Petal C
(cut 6)

Petal B
(cut 8)

Petal A
(cut 10)

creativeedge

page 78

Enlarge 200% or size as desired

Dragon Scale
(cut 10)

dressitup

page 70

Enlarge 200% or size as desired

Collar
(cut 3

Cuffs
(cut 3 sets)

Waistband
(cut 3)

Dress
A

Dress
B

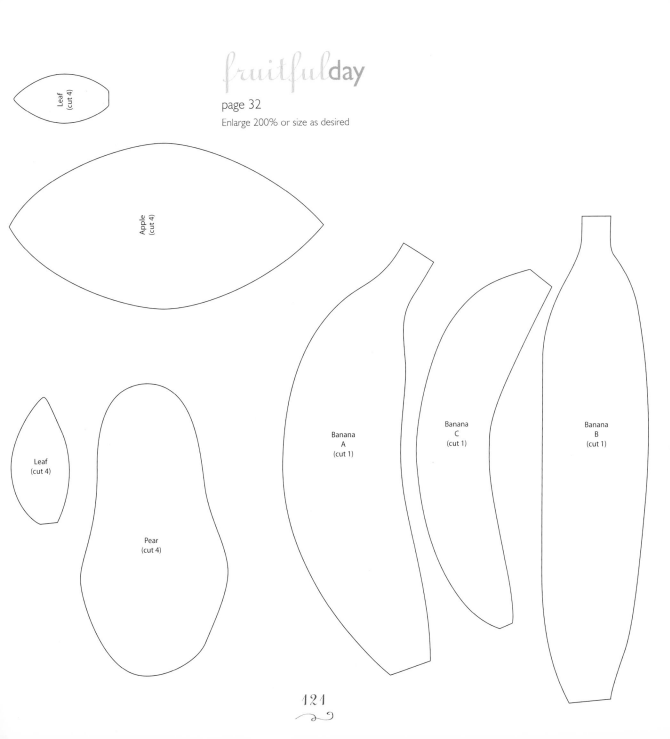

fruitfulday

page 32

Enlarge 200% or size as desired

Leaf
(cut 4)

Apple
(cut 4)

Leaf
(cut 4)

Pear
(cut 4)

Banana
A
(cut 1)

Banana
C
(cut 1)

Banana
B
(cut 1)

cute+curious

page 35

Enlarge 200% or size as desired

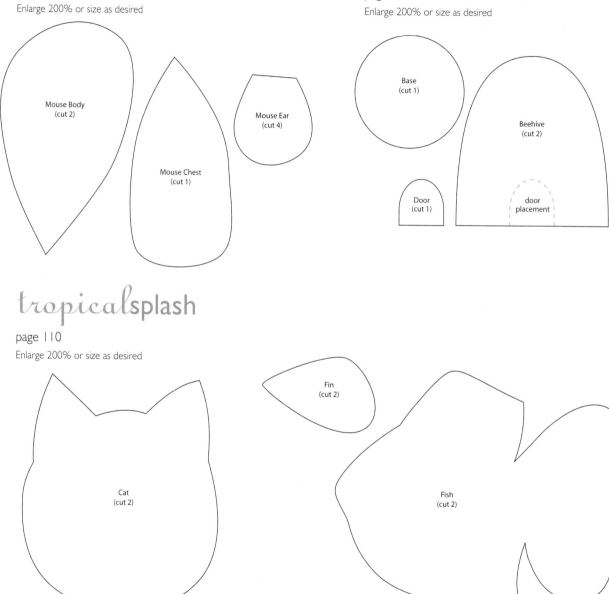

Mouse Body
(cut 2)

Mouse Chest
(cut 1)

Mouse Ear
(cut 4)

beesewing

page 40

Enlarge 200% or size as desired

Base
(cut 1)

Beehive
(cut 2)

Door
(cut 1)

door
placement

tropicalsplash

page 110

Enlarge 200% or size as desired

Cat
(cut 2)

Fin
(cut 2)

Fish
(cut 2)

elegant notions

page 62

Enlarge 200% or size as desired

Edging
(cut 12)

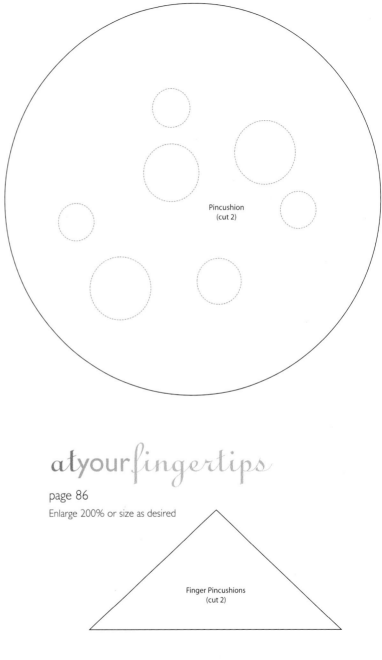

Pincushion
(cut 2)

on pins and needles

page 101

Enlarge 200% or size as desired

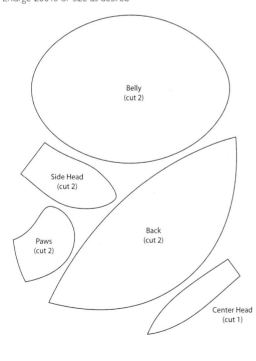

Belly
(cut 2)

Side Head
(cut 2)

Paws
(cut 2)

Back
(cut 2)

Center Head
(cut 1)

at your fingertips

page 86

Enlarge 200% or size as desired

Finger Pincushions
(cut 2)

designsonfelt

page 46

Enlarge 200% or size as desired

Medium Square
(cut 4)

Medium Rectangle
(cut 4)

Small Square
(cut 4)

Small Rectangle
(cut 4)

Side Piece
(cut 4)

Large Square
(cut 3)

Fold

Side Band
(cut 1)

Branch & Leaves
(cut 1 set)

Wing
(cut 1)

Bird
(cut 1)

Large Circle
(cut 3)

Swirl
(cut 1)

Graduated Circles
(cut one set)

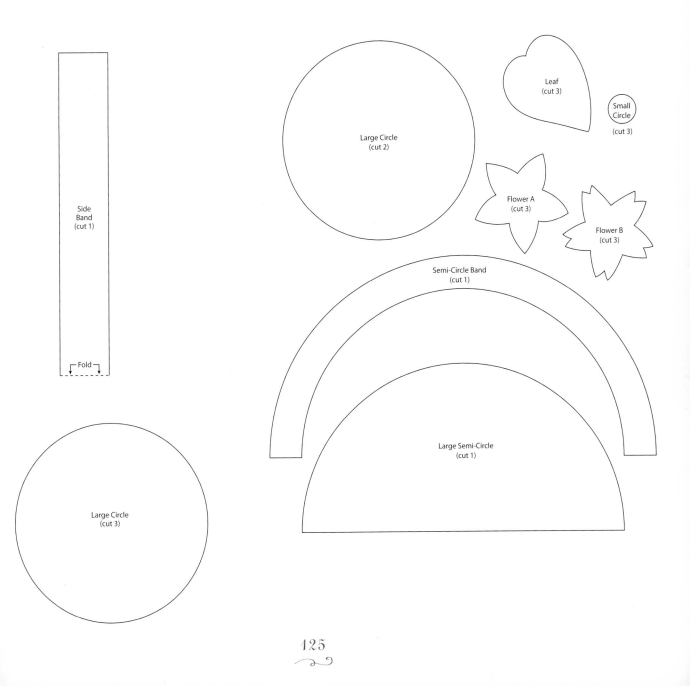

Side
Band
(cut 1)

Fold

Large Circle
(cut 3)

Large Circle
(cut 2)

Leaf
(cut 3)

Small
Circle
(cut 3)

Flower A
(cut 3)

Flower B
(cut 3)

Semi-Circle Band
(cut 1)

Large Semi-Circle
(cut 1)

pinpals

page 106

Enlarge 200% or size as desired

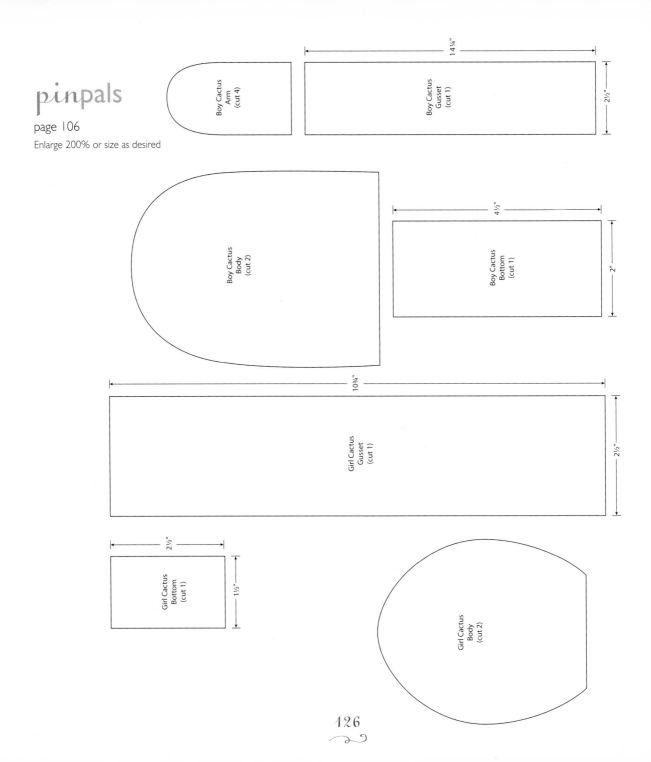

Boy Cactus
Arm
(cut 4)

Boy Cactus
Gusset
(cut 1)

14¼"

2½"

Boy Cactus
Body
(cut 2)

Boy Cactus
Bottom
(cut 1)

4½"

2"

Girl Cactus
Gusset
(cut 1)

10¾"

2½"

Girl Cactus
Bottom
(cut 1)

2½"

1½"

Girl Cactus
Body
(cut 2)

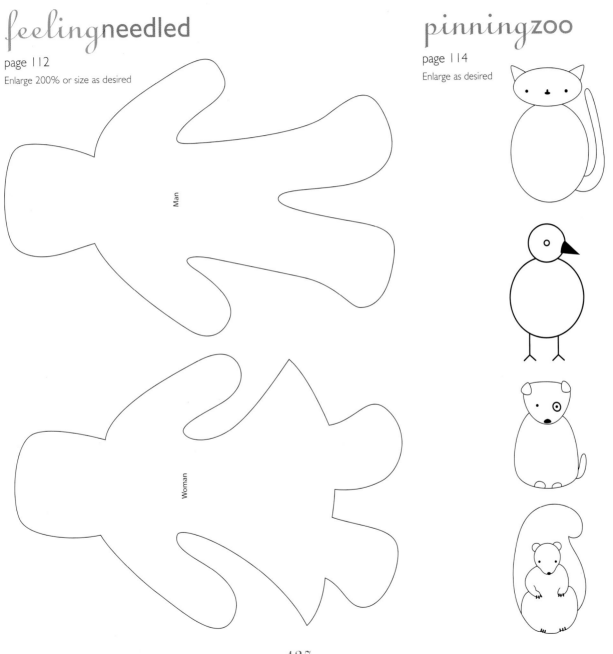

feelingneedled

page 112

Enlarge 200% or size as desired

Man

Woman

pinningzoo

page 114

Enlarge as desired

Index

Acetate alternative, 29
Acknowledgments, 118
Adding scents, 53
Attaching flowers, 94
Basics, 8
Buttons, 56, 94
Cotton, 12
Cutting angles, 72, 105
Cutting curves, 15, 55–56, 105
Douppioni, 64
Embellishments, 14, 83, 94
Fabrics, 12–13, 102
Felt, 13, 56
Felting, 17–18
   sweater selection, 17–18, 108
Flosses, 12
Invisible knot, 45
Leaves, 57, 94
Linen, 12–13
"Losing the thread," 16, 39
Materials, 12–14
Naps, 12–13, 102
Needles, 10–11
Needle threader, 10
Petals, 57, 94
Pins, 10, 42, 83
Pompoms, 57, 94
Rotary cutter, 11
Rounded corners, 15, 55, 56
Scissors, 9
Seam ripper, 10
Sewing machine, 11
Silk, 13, 34, 64
Stitches, 19–21, 93
Stuffing, 13–14, 16, 53, 115
Techniques, 15–21
Threads, 12
Tool kit, 9
Tools, 9–11
Tufting, 16–17
Weaves, 12–13
Weighting, 14, 16

Metric Conversion Chart

INCHES	MILLIMETERS (MM)/ CENTIMETERS (CM)	INCHES	MILLIMETERS (MM)/ CENTIMETERS (CM)
1/8	3 mm	15	38.1 cm
3/16	5 mm	15½	39.4 cm
1/4	6 mm	16	40.6 cm
5/16	8 mm	16½	41.9 cm
3/8	9.5 mm	17	43.2 cm
7/16	1.1 cm	17½	44.5 cm
1/2	1.3 cm	18	45.7 cm
9/16	1.4 cm	18½	47 cm
5/8	1.6 cm	19	48.3 cm
11/16	1.7 cm	19½	49.5 cm
3/4	1.9 cm	20	50.8 cm
13/16	2.1 cm	20½	52 cm
7/8	2.2 cm	21	53.3
15/16	2.4 cm	21½	54.6
1	2.5 cm	22	55 cm
1½	3.8 cm	22½	57.2 cm
2	5 cm	23	58.4 cm
2½	6.4 cm	23½	59.7 cm
3	7.6 cm	24	61 cm
3½	8.9 cm	24½	62.2 cm
4	10.2 cm	25	63.5 cm
4½	11.4 cm	25½	64.8 cm
5	12.7 cm	26	66 cm
5½	14 cm	26½	67.3 cm
6	15.2 cm	27	68.6 cm
6½	16.5 cm	27½	69.9 cm
7	17.8 cm	28	71.1 cm
7½	19 cm	28½	72.4 cm
8	20.3 cm	29	73.7 cm
8½	21.6 cm	29½	74.9 cm
9	22.9 cm	30	76.2 cm
9½	24.1 cm	30½	77.5 cm
10	25.4 cm	31	78.7 cm
10½	26.7 cm	31½	80 cm
11	27.9 cm	32	81.3 cm
11½	29.2 cm	32½	82.6 cm
12	30.5 cm	33	83.8 cm
12½	31.8 cm	33½	85 cm
13	33 cm	34	86.4 cm
13½	34.3 cm	34½	87.6 cm
14	35.6 cm	35	88.9 cm
14½	36.8 cm	35½	90.2 cm
		36	91.4 cm